Surprised by Grace:

MEMORIES AND REFLECTIONS AFTER
25 YEARS OF EPISCOPAL MINISTRY

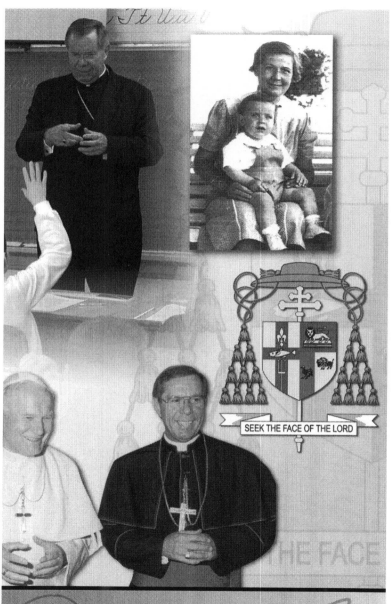

SEEK THE FACE OF THE LORD

Surprised by Grace:

MEMORIES AND REFLECTIONS AFTER
25 YEARS OF EPISCOPAL MINISTRY

THE MOST REVEREND DANIEL M. BUECHLEIN, O.S.B.
Archbishop Emeritus of Indianapolis

Introduction by
Francis Cardinal George, O.M.I
Archbishop of Chicago

Edited by Daniel Conway

Criterion Press, Inc.
Indianapolis

Published by Criterion Press, Inc.
P.O. Box 1717
Indianapolis, IN 46206

ISBN 978-0-578-11557-3

Cover photo by Margaret Nelson
Cover and interior design by Jane Lee

Inside photos by
Criterion file photos by Mary Ann Garber, Sean Gallagher and
Brandon Evans, *Criterion* file photo courtesy *L'Osservatore Romano*,
Criterion file photo courtesy *The West Tennessee Catholic* and
submitted photos from the Buechlein family.

Printed and bound in the United States of America.

IN MEMORIAM

Marguerite (Peg) Knies

This book of memories and reflections after 25 years of episcopal ministry is dedicated to the memory of Marguerite (Peg) Knies, my neighbor, my cousin, my hoped-for sister and my friend, for her courage in the face of cancer. Peg returned to the Lord while praying the rosary with her family. In death, as in life, she was a faithful witness to our Catholic faith.

This publication was made possible by
generous gifts from:

Don and Caryn Mucci
Dan and Beth Elsener
Jerry and Rosie Semler
Tony and Carol Watt
Patrick and Rebecca Carr
Dan and Sharon Conway

TABLE OF CONTENTS

Introduction by Francis Cardinal George, O.M.I. xi

Surprised by Grace: An overview of the Life and
Ministry of Archbishop Daniel M. Buechlein, O.S.B.
by Daniel Conway xiii

Preface xxiii

I   Chapter 1: Aloneness 1

II   Chapter 2: Courage 6

III   Chapter 3: Liberation 10

IV   Chapter 4: Wisdom 15

V   Chapter 5: Family 20

VI   Chapter 6: Work 25

VII   Chapter 7: Charity 30

VIII   Chapter 8: Catechism 35

IX   Chapter 9: Young Adult Ministry 70

X   Chapter 10: Catholic Education 76

XI   Chapter 11: Memphis 84

XII   Chapter 12: Hope 93

XIII   Chapter 13: Mentors 102

XIV   Chapter 14: Saint Meinrad 109

XV   Chapter 15: Stewardship and Development 117

Afterword 129

INTRODUCTION

An introduction to a book of personal reflections over a lifetime's experience is also, to some extent, an introduction to the one who wrote it. While the book speaks for itself, Archbishop Buechlein uses it to speak mostly of others whom the Lord has given him to know and love. He speaks of himself only to draw attention to them, and this is  the attitude of a priest and bishop called to lovingly nurture Christ's own life in the lives of Christ's disciples.

Daniel Mark Buechlein's own life was nurtured by Christ's love, through habits of personal prayer that began as a child in a loving family. His life of prayer was deepened in monastic life and sustained and developed as a bishop of the church in Tennessee and his native Indiana. He is a man of prayer because he is a man of God, as every monk is called to be. He is a man of prayer because he cannot give as a priest what he has not himself received: the love of Christ born in the intimacy of time spent in prayer. He is a man of prayer because prayer raises the curtain between this world and the Kingdom of God, brought to its fullness in the world to come.

We all live in several worlds, often at the same time. Archbishop Buechlein has lived and worked in different places and with different people. The external and changing circumstances of time and place rotated around the internal consistency of his vocation, rooted in the prayer that is the language of God's Kingdom. He lives now in the monastery that was his home for many years, more than ever for him an outpost of that eternal Kingdom.

I will always be grateful for Archbishop Buechlein's invitation to join him and other bishops in the review of catechetical materials for children in our schools and in religious education programs. His personal immersion in the Catholic faith and the theology that is its vehicle made him ideal for the task of leading the bishops in the reform of the instruments necessary to transmit the faith to the next generation. The current Synod of Bishops is discussing the new evangelization for the transmission of the faith, and Archbishop Buechlein's leadership started to prepare this Synod years ago and informs its work today.

The snapshots of his life gathered in this book are a gift to all those who know him or know of him. They will inspire those who have not had the gift of knowing him personally.

Gifts bring us into the future, especially if they are spiritual gifts. Archbishop Buechlein's reflections on the future and on the community we are part of here and hereafter will serve to strengthen the life of faith and prayer in the Church. This book is a gift because his life is a gift from God to him and to the Church.

Francis Cardinal George, O.M.I.
Archbishop of Chicago
October 4, 2012
Feast of St. Francis of Assisi

A Steward of Grace:

An Overview of the Life and Ministry of Archbishop Daniel Mark Buechlein, O.S.B.

Archbishop Daniel M. Buechlein was born in 1938 in the German-American community of Jasper, Ind., and named Marcus George. His parents were Carl and Rose (Blessinger) Buechlein; his father worked 52 years for the Jasper Cabinet Company, and his mother was an elementary school teacher, devoting most of her career to their parish's Holy Family School in Jasper.

The future archbishop attended parochial elementary schools (first St. Joseph School, later Holy Family School when that parish was formed in 1948). He then entered Saint Meinrad High School and College in nearby St. Meinrad, Ind., receiving a Bachelor of Arts degree in philosophy in 1961. While in college, he joined the Benedictine community of Saint Meinrad Archabbey, where he was given the religious name "Daniel." He made his solemn profession as a Benedictine monk in 1962 and was ordained to the priesthood two years later. In 1966, he earned a Licentiate in Sacred Theology from the College of Sant'Anselmo in Rome.

Returning to Saint Meinrad, he served in a number of roles, becoming president-rector of the School of Theology in 1971.

In 1987, Pope John Paul II named him bishop of Memphis and in 1992 appointed him as the eleventh bishop and fifth archbishop of Indianapolis. The websites for the Diocese of Memphis and the Archdiocese of Indianapolis provide brief historical summaries of the contributions made by Daniel Mark Buechlein, O.S.B., during his 5 years as bishop of Memphis and his nearly 20 years as archbishop of Indianapolis. According to the Diocese of Memphis:

> After several months during which Msgr. Paul J. Morris served as Diocesan Administrator, Most Reverend Daniel M. Buechlein assumed the title of Bishop, becoming the first bishop of Memphis to be installed at ceremonies at the Cathedral. He came to Memphis from St. Meinrad Seminary where he had served in several administrative roles in the College and Seminary. He brought great faith and tremendous planning and fund raising skills to his new assignment. Under his tutelage periodic Strategic Plans were developed and adhered to, and the Bishop's Annual Appeal came to be the norm. The planning strategies developed under his leadership provided useful road maps to the diocese's future, and when he left the Diocese of Memphis in 1992 to become Archbishop of Indianapolis, the diocese to which Bishop J. Terry Steib came was in relatively good financial and planning shape.

The Archdiocese of Indianapolis notes the accomplishments of Archbishop Daniel M. Buechlein prior to his retirement in September 2011 as follows:

- Archbishop Buechlein was appointed the fifth Archbishop of Indianapolis on July 14, 1992, by the late Pope John Paul II and was officially installed as archbishop on September 9, 1992. During his episcopacy here, Archbishop Buechlein has worked tirelessly to strengthen the pastoral, spiritual and financial health of the Archdiocese of Indianapolis.

- There are 40 priests in active ministry serving the archdiocese who were ordained by Archbishop Buechlein.

Under Archbishop Buechlein's leadership, the archdiocese:

- Opened Bishop Simon Bruté College Seminary in Indianapolis in 2004 to prepare college seminarians for major seminary. The seminary has already reached its capacity of 35 seminarians and is looking to expand to meet the growing demand.

- Established a Permanent Diaconate program and ordained 25 men as permanent deacons for the archdiocese.

- Raised $300 million through the annual stewardship appeal and separate capital campaigns to pay for building projects and ministry needs throughout the archdiocese. This figure is in excess of the contributions parishioners make through Sunday and Holy Day collections.

- The Catholic Community Foundation, which oversees the archdiocese's endowments, has grown from less than $5 million to its current value of nearly

$170 million. The Catholic Community Foundation now manages nearly 400 endowments. Nearly $70 million from the endowments has been distributed to parishes, schools, and archdiocesan agencies for ministry.

- After a series of significant budget deficits, the archdiocese has attained eight consecutive break-even budgets.
- Expanded the services of Catholic Charities and social outreach ministries of the archdiocese. Last year, the archdiocese's Catholic Charities agencies in central and southern Indiana served nearly 180,000 people. In 2009, after six years of planning and fundraising, the archdiocese opened a new 30,000-square-foot shelter for homeless families. The building named Holy Family Shelter is located next to Holy Trinity Church on the west side of Indianapolis.
- The U.S. Department of Education has awarded 26 of the archdiocese's Catholic schools as with Blue Ribbons in recognition of their excellence. The archdiocese's schools have received more Blue Ribbons than any other diocese in the country.
- Expanded the archdiocese's ministry to young adults by starting a Theology on Tap program and adding new campus ministry programs.
- Initiated the Cause of Beatification and Canonization of Bishop Simon Bruté, the archdiocese's first bishop.
- Celebrated the 175th anniversary of the Archdiocese of Indianapolis [May 5, 2009] with a Mass at Lucas Oil Stadium, which was attended by more than 25,000 people. [The Great Jubilee Mass on September 16,

2000 was attended by more than 30,000 people. That day 3200 youth and adults received the sacrament of Confirmation.]

A much earlier sketch, written by young Mark Buechlein when he was in the fifth grade at St. Joseph School in Jasper, Ind., and titled "The History of My Life," summarizes the earliest known facts about his life:

I was born Wednesday, April 20, 1938, at 10:30 a.m. at our present home in Little Kentucky near Jasper, Indiana. My mother was Rose Blessinger and my father is Carl Buechlein.

I was baptized on April 21, 1938, at 5 p.m. in St. Joseph's Church by Father James Reed, O.S.B. My Godparents were my father's brother, George Buechlein and my mother's sister, Agnes Stenftenagle. I was given the name Marcus George.

I had my first tooth October 20, 1938, and by April 20, 1939, my first birthday, I had sixteen teeth.

I took my first step while visiting near Champagne, Ill., June 14, 1939. My family went there to attend First Communion services for my cousin Rosemary Wagner. My first words were "mama," "dada," and "lala" which meant mother, father and Charlie, my brother.

Some of my early memories were not pleasant because there was war. I don't remember when it began, but I was very happy when it ended.

I also remember when my uncle sold his farm and rented our upstairs until he built his new home.

Mother says I didn't get into serious mischief when I was small but many people had to take care of me because my mother was ill.[1]

I started to school in September 1944 at the Bockelman country school. My first day was my best and easiest. My teacher was my uncle Adam Blessinger. He also taught my second year.

Country school was much different, all classes studied and recited in the same room. I always wanted to listen in on all classes and sometimes I forgot to do my lessons. In second grade I didn't miss a day of school and I got a nice eversharp for a prize. I was proud of it. I made my best grade this year also.

I made my First Holy Communion on October 28, 1945.

In the third grade I started to attend St. Joseph's School. My teacher was Sister Ann Denise.[2] Everything was strange. It took me a while to get used to the different routine but after a while I liked it.

In the fourth grade I joined the choir. I enjoy this because I like music. Sister Marie Annette was my teacher and I liked her very much. It was this year that they planned on building a new school and church. It was to be Holy Family Parish.

---

[1] Mark Buechlein learned later—not from his mother—that his birth had been a difficult one and that Rose Buechlein believed that this was a sign her son was destined to do great things.

[2] Sister Ann Denise was the first teacher to suggest to Mark Buechlein that he had a vocation to the priesthood.

In the fifth grade my teachers are Sister Louise Marie and Sister Marie Cicele. This year is different because we change class for English, the class I am writing this for now.

Two big things happened this year. St. Joseph School was struck by lightning on January 4, 1949. The other thing is The Holy Family School, which I probably will be attending next year, is beginning to look like something.

Marcus George Buechlein was a member of the first class to graduate from Holy Family School in Jasper, Ind., in the spring of 1952. Several months later, he entered the minor seminary at Saint Meinrad. As noted above, after being given the religious name "Daniel" he made his solemn vows as a monk in August 1962, was ordained a priest two years later, and served as a teacher, spiritual director and eventually rector of Saint Meinrad Seminary for 23 years until Pope John Paul II appointed him bishop of Memphis in January 1987 at the age of 48.

When he was ordained a bishop in Memphis on March 2, 1987, after serving as a monk and priest of Saint Meinrad Archabbey for nearly 25 years, Daniel Mark Buechlein told the clergy, religious and faithful of his new diocese that his first duty as a bishop was to be a man of prayer. He repeated that pledge five years later when he was installed as archbishop of Indianapolis on September 9.

Archbishop Buechlein never forgets that prayer is his primary responsibility. In fact, as he told the clergy, religious and faithful who attended his last official meeting as chief shepherd of the Church in central and southern Indiana, "I'm not quitting." Shortly afterward, he returned to his roots in southern Indiana to continue and intensify the ministry of prayer that he first embraced as a monk of Saint Meinrad nearly 50 years ago and that he has accepted as his primary responsibility as a bishop.

According to the *Catechism of the Catholic Church* (#893), "the bishop is the steward of grace of the supreme priesthood especially in the Eucharist. ..." The phrase "steward of grace" is an especially apt description of Archbishop Buechlein because of his spirituality and his administrative skill. The catechism goes on to say that "bishops and priests sanctify the Church by their prayer and work, by their ministry of the word and of the sacraments. They sanctify her by their example, not as domineering over those in [their] charge but by being examples to the flock" (cf. 1 Pt 5:3).

As this book of memories and reflections on his 25 years of episcopal ministry makes clear, Archbishop Buechlein takes his responsibilities seriously. Formed by loving parents who practiced their faith with deep devotion and who lovingly handed it on to their two sons, the young Mark Buechlein was well-prepared for the education and training he received at Saint Meinrad. *Ora et labora,* prayer and work, is a centuries-old Benedictine motto. Through the teaching and example of his monastic confrères, Father Daniel, as he was known then, grew to appreciate and put into practice the style of life that is sometimes called "contemplation in action." Even as a young monk, he was very busy—teaching, counseling, providing spiritual direction and serving as an administrator skilled at planning, motivating and delegating. But because he is first and foremost a man of prayer, the active life he lived as a seminary rector, bishop and metropolitan archbishop never interfered with his ministry of word and sacrament or his commitment to sanctify by example. "I am called to be a man of prayer," he says. "It's my main job."

I have been privileged to know Archbishop Buechlein for 45 years. He was my freshman hall dean at Saint Meinrad College. He taught me philosophy, liturgy and the sacraments. He was our director of spiritual formation in college, and afterward, when I attended the graduate School of Theology, he was president-rector. Later I worked for him—first in the development office at Saint Meinrad and then in the Archdiocese of Indianapolis. He is the best administrator—and one of the best fundraisers—I have ever known. What is the secret of his success as a spiritual leader, manager of the Church's temporal affairs and "steward of grace of the supreme priesthood"? I can say without hesitation that he is successful because he is first and foremost a man of prayer.

Archbishop Buechlein's early retirement is a bittersweet experience for all of us who have had the privilege of working closely with him over the years. When he was first installed as archbishop, he was a vigorous young man of 54, a runner whose boundless energy made him impossible to keep up with. Age and illness have changed him before our eyes (as happened to Blessed John Paul II). That, too, is a part of the witness that popes and bishops now are called to give to a world that disdains aging and suffering as it vainly seeks to remain forever young.

Archbishop Buechlein requested, and received, Pope Benedict XVI's blessing to give up his active duties as a bishop. No more planning, personnel management, budget-cutting or fundraising! But he did not ask to be relieved of his primary responsibility—to be a man of prayer.

We miss the archbishop's active leadership, but it should be a great consolation to all of us to know—with absolute certainty—that he is not quitting. He remains a steward of grace whose ministry is to be a man prayer and an example of obedient acceptance to God's will no matter what the cost.

Daniel Conway
Editor

PREFACE

On the evening of March 18, 2011, I looked forward to the next day's celebration of the Solemnity of St. Joseph. My plan was to spend the holy day visiting the retired priests of our archdiocese, Blessed Teresa of Calcutta's sisters (the Missionaries of Charity) and the Little Sisters of the Poor. It was to be a full day, and I was looking forward to it.

After saying my evening prayers and doing a little reading, I retired early (about 8:30 p.m.). I was tired, but I felt pretty well considering the physical challenges of the past several years and my recovery from cancer, shoulder surgery and various other health problems. As I say, I was looking forward to a full day dedicated to St. Joseph, one of my favorite saints.

God had other plans for me. At around 3:30 in the morning, I woke up and realized with a start that something was very wrong. I stood up and immediately went into a kind of tailspin. I lunged at my bed in an attempt to break my fall. Thank God, it worked, and I made a soft landing on my bed!

From my bed, I was able to reach for the telephone, call 911 and give the emergency dispatcher enough information so that she could call for help. Although I didn't know for sure, I guessed that I had had a stroke, and I knew that fast action is very important for stroke victims.

Once I knew the paramedics were on their way, I had to figure out how to unlock the front door so they could get in. Somehow I managed to crawl out of the bedroom and down the stairs to the front door mumbling prayers to St. Joseph to help me. I reached up, unlocked the door and then crawled back to the stairs where I sat down and waited for the response team.

I'm very grateful to the paramedics who came and helped me. They placed me on a gurney and took me to St. Vincent Hospital in an ambulance. I received good care at St. Vincent and at the rehab facility in Indianapolis, but it was clear that God's plan for me was very different from my plans that day and in the weeks, months and years ahead.

On March 19, 2011, the Solemnity of St. Joseph, my life changed forever. I had to surrender that day to God's will for me. I had to abandon my plans and go where the Lord was leading me. I had to take up my particular cross and follow him without knowing or understanding where he was—and is—leading me.

I'm grateful that this radical change in my life happened on the feast of St. Joseph. He himself had plans that were radically altered—more than once—by divine intervention. He always said "yes" even when he didn't understand.

I pray that St. Joseph will intercede for me, and inspire me, as I learn to accept God's will in my life. And I offer the following memories and reflections on my 25 years of episcopal ministry (and 74 years of life) as a gift to all the wonderful family members, friends and co-workers who walk with me in the final stages of my life's journey.

During his 85th birthday homily, Pope Benedict XVI, one of my heroes, said, "I am in the final stage of my life journey and I do not know what awaits me. However, I do know that the light of God exists, that He rose again, that

His light is stronger than all darkness, that the goodness of God is stronger than all the evil in this world. This helps me to continue with confidence. This helps us to continue, and I would like to thank everyone who, through their faith, continually makes me aware of God's yes."

I couldn't say it any better. I don't know what awaits me, but I believe with all my heart and mind and strength, that I am in God's hands. This helps me to continue with confidence, with gratitude and, yes, with joy.

+Daniel Mark Buechlein, O.S.B.
Archbishop Emeritus of Indianapolis
Saint Meinrad Archabbey
May 8, 2012

CHAPTER ONE

ALONENESS

When I first awoke after the stroke, I experienced a profound sense of aloneness. I knew immediately that, from now on, everything would be different—my mind, my body and my emotions. Everything was changed for me, and I knew that I had to come to terms with my total dependence on others. I had to learn how to be alone with God.

I have been blessed with deep friendships during my 25 years as a bishop and also during my days as a student, teacher and seminary rector. Friends are a gift from God that we too often take for granted. I treasure the letters, phone calls and personal visits I have had since my stroke. But the profound sense of aloneness remains.

Before Blessed Pope John Paul II called me to be the bishop of Memphis in 1987, I had the privilege of belonging to a community of monks whose mission is to seek God through their prayer and work. The monks of Saint Meinrad Archabbey welcomed me back after 25 years away, and they have been very good to me.

Today everyone thinks that "community" is the answer to everything, but the Holy Rule of St. Benedict cautions against that kind of thinking. Each monk is called to seek God alone. The support of the community, the monastic liturgy (*Opus Dei*), holy reading (*Lectio Divina*), common work and meals and the fraternity of the monks are all important dimensions of the "school of the Lord's service" that is the Benedictine way of life. But in the end, each monk seeks God alone.

The stroke has forced me to come to terms with that in new ways.

On the occasion of my 25th anniversary as a bishop, my good friend Archbishop J. Peter Sartain preached at Vespers in the Archabbey Church. He said:

> The life of a priest is very busy. But there is nothing as relentless as the call of the Gospel; nothing as persistent as the demands of love; nothing as unyielding as the faithfulness of God; nothing as unrelentingly piercing as the gaze of God; nothing as relentless as God's seeking, God's searching, for the lost sheep, for sinners like us; nothing as relentless as God's desiring to save us and bring us home. And thus, for the monk, for the seminarian, for the deacon, for the priest, and for the bishop, there is nothing more important than seeking, and seeking relentlessly, the One who seeks us.

My challenge is still to seek God relentlessly, but my search must be carried out in new ways. I am no longer "busy" the way I was before the stroke. My ministry now is one of prayer and daily monastic witness wherever I am. And, yet, I am working harder than ever to be a faithful disciple of Jesus Christ, to surrender to the will of the Father, to regain my physical strength, to channel my emotions, and to use my mind to pray, to learn and to teach. In short, I continue to seek God in the dramatically changed circumstances of my life and ministry.

It's not a cakewalk. Some days it's extraordinarily difficult and painful. I fall periodically. When I stand up, my blood pressure plummets, and I lose my balance. The last time this happened, I sustained a concussion. Thank God I have wonderful caregivers who prevent me from falling, or who catch me as I'm about to hit the ground, or who pick me up after I've fallen and check to make sure I don't have another concussion or a broken bone. It's hard to be so dependent on other people, but what a blessing it is to have them so close at hand when I need them!

Since the stroke, I have had to face the fact that I will never be able to live on my own again. My emotions, and my pride, strongly reject this humiliating truth about myself. I know that I have to fight against the temptation to see myself as "damaged goods for life." In fact, that's not the case at all. My mind is clear. My body is healing. And I'm learning to deal with my emotions.

I'm not damaged goods. I'm a monk, a priest and a bishop who seeks God alone. I am relentlessly seeking the One who seeks me, as Archbishop Sartain said, in the new circumstances of my life.

One of the most precious gifts I received on my 25th anniversary of episcopal ordination was a framed personal message and photograph from Pope Benedict XVI. The Holy Father knows me from the days when he was prefect of the Congregation for the Doctrine of the

Faith and I was chairman of the U. S. bishops' Committee on the Implementation of the *Catechism of the Catholic Church*. Pope Benedict's anniversary greeting reads:

> We heartily congratulate our venerable brother, Daniel Mark Buechlein, O.S.B., Archbishop Emeritus of Indianapolis, as he observes the silver jubilee of his episcopal consecration. We are happy with his pastoral assiduity for the spiritual welfare of the faithful entrusted to his care, carried out as he sought the face of the Lord (Ps 105:4). We wish him divine solace and we lovingly bestow on him our apostolic blessing, harbinger of heavenly graces yet to come. (From the Vatican the 8th day of September 2012, Benedict XVI)

When I first read this, my eyes went immediately to the phrase "harbinger of graces yet to come" and I thought to myself, "O Lord, what else do you have in store for me? Does the Holy Father know something that I don't?"

Fortunately, I believe that everyone receives heavenly graces from God, and these gifts and blessings can take many different forms. So, whatever challenges come my way—now and in the future—I pray for the strength, and the humility, to accept them as heavenly graces the way our Lord accepted the Father's will for him.

As Jesus says so poignantly in St. John's Gospel, "Whoever serves me must follow me… . I am troubled now. Yet what should I say? 'Father, save me from this hour'? But it was for this purpose that I came to this hour" (cf. Jn 20:20-33).

I became a monk, a priest and a bishop in order to

seek God. Now God has asked me to seek him in new ways. I'm occasionally troubled by this, but what should I say? Father, save me from this hour? No, this is God's will for me now, and like it or not, I must obey.

One day not long ago when I was praying in the Archabbey Church, a group of young people came in for a visit. One of the teenage boys looked closely at me as he passed. Then he said, "I know you. You're the old one." He meant that I was the former archbishop—the one who confirmed him, but I said, "Yes. I'm the old one. Please pray for me."

CHAPTER TWO

COURAGE

During my 25 years as a bishop, one of my top priorities has been ministry to the young Church. Wherever I was—celebrating the sacrament of confirmation, speaking at youth conferences, on college or seminary campuses or participating in informal gatherings at my residence—I made a point of telling young people that we need them, we love them and we support them.

My whole approach has always been to support young people and encourage them to want to serve in the Church, not only as priests and religious but also as lay witnesses to their Catholic faith. Our youth need and deserve the witness of sacrificial love. I have no doubt in my mind that, given the guidance and support they need, our young Church will respond to a prophetic, counter-cultural way of living because our youth are looking for a life of meaning and love that is real.

In his Holy Rule, St. Benedict admonishes the senior members of the monastic community to listen to younger members. Youth often have important things to teach us older people. Sometimes their insights are fresher and more "on point" than our own world-weary thoughts and attitudes.

I was given a powerful experience of this truth when I was in recovery from Hodgkin's lymphoma several years ago. During that time I received many homemade get-well cards from students in our archdiocese's schools and parish religious education programs. I will never forget one letter I received from a young fellow named Bryan.

"My name is Bryan. I go to St. Roch Catholic School. I am 12 years old and in the sixth grade. I play football and basketball there. My favorite sport is basketball. My favorite subject is Social Studies. My favorite extracurricular activity is Spell Bowl. My favorite football team is the Giants."

Then, as I turned to the back page, I discovered this extraordinary entry under the title "Courage." He wrote:

"The definition of courage is hard to memorize. But luckily for everyone, it's easy to describe. It's the ability to move forward when times are dark. The times you give it all you got, even though you're weary. So remember dear Archbishop, that even though times are bad, you've still got the grace of God, so always stay glad. Sincerely, Bryan Rush."

I was touched and impressed by Bryan's profound and appropriate message.

In many ways, this young man helped me accept the fact that my cancer was God's gift. It was an opportunity to pause, to evaluate my ministry as an archbishop and to appreciate anew the goodness of God's loving grace. Bryan's call to courage underscored what I knew I needed to do. His insight provided a fine stimulus for me to remember that Easter comes by way of the cross. There is no other way.

In the Scripture readings after Easter, we read of the courage of the apostles and disciples after Christ's resurrection and ascension.

St. John Chrysostom wrote: "They ignored the danger of death ... they forgot how few they were; they never noticed how many were against them or the power or strength or wisdom of their enemies. Their power was greater than all that: theirs was the power of him who had died on the cross and risen again" (Homilies on St. Matthew, 4).

In 1985, Pope John Paul II wrote a letter to the youth of the world. Speaking to the young people of that time, he told them how tremendously important their teenage years were because, during this time of their lives, they were beginning to take personal responsibility for their decisions and to make choices about their future. Young people deal with the questions "What does God want for me?" and "What can I do to make a difference in this world?"

The Holy Father's advice was very powerful. He told the young Church: "As you search for answers to answer these all-important questions about the meaning of your life and the world we live in, look to Christ. If you pray every day in your own way, everything will be OK. You'll find yourself a lot more peaceful, a lot happier and a long way down the road toward figuring out what you can be and do to make a difference in life."

I believe that our challenge as disciples is to bravely carry the cross of Christ. I'm very optimistic about the future of the Church. If we keep the faith, look to Christ, pray the Our Father, and purify our relationship with God, everything will be OK.

In December 2001, I welcomed more than 20,000

Catholic teenagers from throughout the United States and three foreign countries to the National Catholic Youth Conference in Indianapolis. On that occasion, I said to the young people, "Without any doubt, some of you are called to be courageous priests and religious women for the new millennium. To be sure, all of you are called to stand up for Christ. Yours is the challenge to keep yourselves alert to God's inspiration and to grow strong in your faith. A sure way to keep alert to God's inspiration is to develop the practice, the habit, of personal prayer. You'll be surprised by the spiritual power of God's grace.

At the time that I said this, I had no idea how surprised I would be several years later by the crosses I would be called to carry through my cancer, my shoulder surgery and my stroke. Thank God for the spiritual power of God's grace and for the advice I received from a 6th grader at St. Roch School who reminded me to "always stay glad."

Gladness in the face of suffering is not something superficial. In fact, there is nothing more profound. At the heart of Christian faith is the powerful truth that Easter comes by way of the cross. There is no other way.

Sometimes when I'm awake in the early morning hours, I make the Way of the Cross. Young Bryan Rush reminded me that courage can be described as moving forward with faith, hope and charity even when times are bad. "The times you give it all you got, even though you're weary."

Surely that's what our Lord did when he carried his cross to Calvary. Surely this is what all of us are called to do—sustained by the power of God's grace and grateful for the gift of his love.

CHAPTER THREE

LIBERATION

On Wednesday of Holy Week 2012, I participated in the monastic community's communal celebration of the sacrament of the anointing of the sick along with several other monks who are elderly or infirm. As we read in the *Catechism of the Catholic Church* (#1531), "The celebration of the Anointing of the Sick consists essentially in the anointing of the forehead and hands of the sick person (in the Roman Rite) or of other parts of the body (in the Eastern rite), the anointing being accompanied by the liturgical prayer of the celebrant asking for the special grace of this sacrament."

This beautiful sacrament is not just for those who are close to death. Anyone who is seriously ill may receive the grace of this sacrament as often as this particular gift of the Holy Spirit is needed to bring comfort, healing, courage and inner peace.

When I received this sacrament during this Holy Week, I asked myself: What can I realistically expect in the way of healing? Can I expect a miraculous cure? Can I anticipate that the effects of my stroke will disappear overnight? With God all things are possible, and I can always hope and pray for an immediate, complete recovery, but these are not realistic expectations for me.

What kind of healing can I realistically expect from the manifold graces of the anointing of the sick?

The answer that came to me in prayer is "liberation"—freedom from the domination of pain and infirmity. The greatest temptation that sick people have is to give in to hopelessness and despair. Self-absorption is a consequence of intense pain and suffering. The danger is that we will think only of ourselves, of our suffering and our aloneness. For many of us who are ill, healing includes "letting go" of our preoccupation with self and "giving back to the Lord" the depression and discomfort that are the consequences of our illnesses—whatever they happen to be.

One Easter, Blessed Pope John Paul II prayed that the Risen Christ would receive into his glorified wounds all the painful wounds of contemporary society. He meant those wounds we read and hear so much about in the news media, and also those that weigh heavily, and silently, on so many people's hearts. It is a rare Easter Sunday that does not find strife in our contentious world, and painful wounds among us!

I pray that my reception of the sacrament of the anointing of the sick helps me hand over to the Risen Christ the suffering that I have been asked to endure. I'm convinced that if I'm successful, I will experience the elation—the overwhelming sense of liberation—that Christ alone can give. The elation that comes as a pure gift from God cannot be bought or borrowed. It is one of the surprises that we experience as a result of grace. It has nothing to do with what we ourselves have accomplished or achieved.

As I think about this experience of liberation (*elation* is not exactly the right word, but it comes close), I remember other times in my life when I have felt this way. Three occasions come to mind: the day I made my solemn profession of vows as a monk of Saint Meinrad Archabbey, my ordination to the priesthood, and my episcopal consecration. Each of these occasions involved a kind of death, a handing over of self that entailed a renunciation of worldly freedoms in exchange for a particular commitment of myself to the Lord's service (with no strings attached).

The afternoon of my solemn profession of monastic vows I remember feeling light-hearted and affirmed by the Lord. I experienced a deep-seated sense of peace and joy that I had never known before.

Ordination to the priesthood was a similar experience, a confirmation that I was following the path laid out for me by Christ. My consecration as a bishop was accompanied by a nearly overwhelming sense of my unworthiness, but I had no fear, no lack of confidence in the power of God's grace to sustain me. As a result, the elation I felt that day was very powerful.

In each case, I knew with absolute certainty that the elation I was experiencing was not the result of my own achievement. It was grace, a gift from God that I did not deserve but that would carry me forward into an unknown future.

Pope Benedict XVI's apostolic exhortation on the Eucharist, "The Sacrament of Charity," relates the Eucharist and the anointing of the sick. "Jesus did not only send his disciples forth to heal the sick; he also instituted a specific sacrament for them: the anointing of the sick. … If the Eucharist shows how Christ's suffering and death have been transformed into love, the anointing of the sick, for its part, unites the sick with Christ's self-offering for the salvation of all, so that they too, within the mystery of the communion of saints, can participate in the redemption of all" (n. 22). This means that the sick are not simply passive recipients of the grace of the sacrament. The Holy Father says that by giving back to the Lord our pain, our suffering and our physical and emotional wounds, we *participate in Christ's redemptive mission*!

This is a message that I want to share with others. I have a cousin named Peg who was like a sister to me growing up. She has pancreatic cancer now, and as I listen to her concerns I am filled with the desire to share with her and many, many others the hope, and the healing power, of Jesus. I want to give back to the Lord all my suffering— not for my own sake but so that I can give witness to the liberating power of God's grace.

The *Catechism of the Catholic Church* (#1520) teaches us that the first grace of the sacrament of the anointing of the sick "is one of strengthening, peace and courage to overcome the difficulties that go with the condition of serious illness or the frailty of old age. This grace is a gift of the Holy Spirit, who renews trust and faith in God and strengthens against the temptations of the evil one, the temptation to discouragement and anguish in the face of death. This assistance from the Lord by the power of his Spirit is meant to lead the sick person to healing of the soul, but also of the body if such is God's will."

Easter peace is ours to receive from Christ. Let's not miss the crucial fact that it is mediated through the Church, especially through the sacraments of penance, the Eucharist and the anointing of the sick—sacraments made possible by holy orders. And so, yes, Easter peace is always available to us in and through the sacraments of the Church.

Let's share this extraordinary peace, this genuine feeling of liberation and elation in response to the undeserved gift of God's grace, with all who are suffering—mentally, physically or emotionally.

CHAPTER FOUR

WISDOM

One of my favorite photos of my mother, Rose Bless-inger Buechlein, was taken at a diocesan teacher's conference in Evansville. She happened to be in the center of the photo looking as serene as I always remember her. I suspect it was this characteristic that caught the photographer's attention.

Of course, there were times when she would be distressed, particularly if she happened on to gossip. She would have nothing to do with rumors and judgmental anecdotes often passed around in common conversation. Mom taught me that gossip, and the envy that underlies it, is especially destructive to individuals and communities. Gossip ruins reputations and causes talented people to "hold back" out of human respect so as to avoid the risk of being talked about in vicious ways.

As a young woman, before her marriage and beginning a family, Mom taught in one-room public schools in Dubois County, Ind. In fact, she taught the young man who later became her pastor at Holy Family Parish in Jasper, Ind. He eventually hired her as the first lay teacher in the parish school.

I would visit my mom's classroom once a semester during my time at Saint Meinrad. Usually, she would have me there during religion class, and it was a treat to interact with the fourth graders. Of course, I am biased as I look back with fond memories, but I was inevitably impressed by the responsiveness of her students and by the knowledge they gained from her teaching.

I remember that so many of her former students came by to pay their respects at the calling prior to her funeral. Many were at the funeral Mass as well.

I was reminded of the impact that teachers can have on our youth and young adults. I still run into former grade school students of hers who make a point of telling me how much they appreciated being in her classroom.

As I think back to my grade school education, I respect Mom greatly for the manner in which she allowed me to make my way on my own. One might expect that, being a teacher, she would have constantly been looking over my shoulder to keep me on track. She did it from afar, and I never felt pressured by her. I would ascribe that to her wisdom.

Twice in her later years, Mom fell and broke a hip. I thought back to those years when I had my bout with Hodgkin's lymphoma and, more recently, when I needed a shoulder replacement and when I had to do physical therapy after my stroke. I fixed on her manner of accepting physical problems as they came, and keeping her calmness intact while she was determined to do the difficult rehabilitation.

My sister-in-law, Marge, was a faithful attendant to Mom in her rehabilitation. When Marge was away, once in awhile I tried to step in and work with Mom. I remember hoping at the time that some day I would be as quietly persevering against tough physical challenges. I haven't been as successful at staying calm and maintaining my serenity as Mom was, but her example inspires me to do better.

Memories of her witness have helped me with my health issues. That her rosary was always nearby in her waning years did not escape my attention.

I would not have dared to write these few thoughts if Mom were still alive. She never wanted to be the center of attention!

I remember washing dishes with Mom after dinner one night when I was still in grade school. I had brought home a good report card and some Boy Scout honors, and I asked her if it was OK to enjoy my achievements. She smiled at me and said, "Yes, Mark. You can enjoy your achievements—as long as you remember that you didn't do these things all by yourself."

Mom taught elementary school, but not once did she do my homework. If I had questions, she was there for me. She did keep an eye on me so that I did what I was supposed to do. And she would pat me on the back when I brought home a good report card.

With hindsight, I appreciate the fact that she gave me room to develop the habit of taking initiative for my responsibilities in life. As I grew older, I found that I was not the only one to recognize that, in a quiet way, Mom was a source of extraordinary wisdom. One of my priest-friends regularly called to mind her calm and steady manner—and her wisdom.

The older I am, the more I appreciate the values that

Mom and Dad passed on to my brother and me. One of those was the value and dignity of hard work. Only later in life, especially as I read some of the social encyclicals of our more recent popes, I recognized that although they didn't say it, our folks were teaching us that work is one of the ways in which we experience our human dignity.

Our parents taught us the Catholic faith and provided us with the education to understand and appreciate the sacraments and the doctrines of the Church. They taught us by the simple example of their lives as well as with timely words along the way.

As I write this book in 2012, looking back on my 74 years of life, I am so grateful for the blessings of having such a wonderful family. Mom and Dad were truly my teachers in life and in faith. With afterthought, I would say they may have taught me more by the way they lived than by what they told me.

Two challenges from my parents served me well in learning to live in a community of like-minded men. Mom taught me never to claim privileges for myself that every other person in the group could not claim. She reminded me that I am no better nor more privileged than the next person because we are all God's children.

And Dad drummed into my head that "a job worth doing is worth doing well." But most of all, my parents taught me to pray and to be willing to serve. They did so until they could do no more.

As I struggle with my current physical and emotional challenges, I pray that I might emulate the humility, generosity and serenity of my Mom and Dad. I am so conscious of the gifts that my brother and I received growing up! I pray that I can follow their example—to be willing to pray, and to serve, until I can do no more.

CHAPTER FIVE

FAMILY

In the back of my favorite Bible, I have kept a note written to me by my mom as she was recovering from replacement of a broken hip. She wrote:

"Dear Mark, Aunt Mary says her accident happened for a reason. I'm sure mine did, too. I can't tell you how much it made me realize what our family means to me.

"I'll never forget that after causing everyone so much misery I awoke and saw you kneeling by my bed!! (I had been in Arizona.) I couldn't imagine how much extra effort it took to get you there.

"Thank you for all the nights you slipped in to comfort me in my misery. We don't really know how lucky we are for having such a fine family.

"May God bless you, and we thank you for all the prayers and help."

Mom believed that accidents (and illnesses) happen for a reason. She had a profound faith in the Providence of God. She believed that her hip fracture was an occasion of grace—a chance to pause and reflect on how important family is.

Mom and Dad passed on to my brother and me their

deep love and respect for God's gift of family life. How grateful we both are for the blessings of a good family!

I've been thinking a lot about my dad lately. He was the strong one, always in the background taking care of Mom in her illnesses. And what strikes me so strongly these days is that my dad never, ever asked for a thing.

I can't remember a time that he wasn't self-effacing—even when he was in his own final illness. His life was given to hard and steady work, and presence for his wife and sons and, also, members of our extended family.

It occurs to me how our dads who are like that make it so easy to take them for granted.

I must admit that with hindsight I regret that I couldn't spend more time with him in his last year or so, even though he wouldn't have remembered. Of course, he is very much with me in my thoughts and prayers now.

It is a blessed family that can give thanks to God for parents who have been and are able to nurture their marriage and a wonderful family through the good times and the bad. In contrast to the secular phenomenon of serial marriages or simply couples living together without the covenant of marriage, what marvelous witness fidelity in marriage is in our times.

The annual archdiocesan celebration of couples who have been married 50, 60 and more years has always been one of my favorite events. The assembly is radiant. No couple, no matter how deep their love is on the day of their marriage, can make it through the good times and the bad, through sickness and health until death without the grace of God. And so couples come to church on their wedding day to ask for God's help. Couples come to ask God to be a third partner in their married life. However romantic their wedding day may have been, mature couples realize that they need God's help.

If a wife and husband want to have a blessed family life, they never give up going to church, faithfully, regularly, in the hard times and in the good times, when convenient or inconvenient. Blessed couples are people of simple faith, and they are also as down-to-earth and hardworking and fun-loving as any people you can find.

Many centuries ago, St. John Chrysostom gave the following advice to Christian men (and to couples): "Show your wife you appreciate her company a lot and that you prefer to be home rather than outside, because she is there. Show her a preference among all your friends and even above the children she has given you; love them because of her. ... Pray all together, ... Learn the fear of God; everything else will flow from this like water from a fountain and your house will be filled with bounty" (Twentieth homily on the Letter to the Ephesians).

Of course, this famous Church preacher intended this advice for husband and wife mutually.

But the generous love of a married couple extends beyond the family home, within the limits of possibility, of course. When extended family or neighbors or strangers are in trouble, a generous couple is there, even at great cost, even if it hurts to get there. That's how God's grace works out in a faithful Christian married life. The vocation within Christian marriage is to be a sacrament, a channel of God's love to neighbor. And Christ enlarged the meaning of family to include the neighbor in need.

It works the other way around as well. God's grace

comes home for wife and husband in the sacrament of marriage through family and friends and others who reach out their love to them. God's grace doesn't come home only in church and at formal prayer. It comes through the people around us, too.

Marriage is a sacrament of love lived in the real world. Sometimes married love may be hard work. It will not always be lived perfectly, but where love is grounded in faith and enriched by God's grace, even in difficulties, there can be beauty and deep meaning in life.

Blessed Teresa of Calcutta used to say that loneliness is the worst poverty in the United States. Families that support one another—and their neighbors and friends—respond to this spiritual poverty in important ways.

Did not Jesus intend that the celebration of the body and blood of Christ should draw families together, and that the family should be the place of our salvation against the chaos and the confusion that is still so much a part of our world?

In a world of broken families, surely Jesus wanted us, his Church, to be family, a community of faith. And surely Jesus intended that our homes should be the cells which form the family that is the Church. And so every time we receive the holy Eucharist, the body and blood of Christ and the sacrament of unity and charity, we participate in a celebration of the one family of God.

At the holy Eucharist, we are to welcome those who need us to be family for them. We are to welcome each other because we need to be family for each other—in our homes and in our churches. The Eucharist makes us a community to which we can belong, even when we are alone.

Let's pray for the grace to come together as family, and as a family of families, so that we never have to be lonely, frightened or alone again.

CHAPTER SIX

WORK

Labor Day weekend always brings to mind my dad, who was born on Sept. 4, 1906, and died near his 90th birthday. Particularly in his early years, and especially during the Great Depression, his life was not easy. He worked hard to make a life for my mom, brother and me.

As for everyone else, things didn't always go the way he would have liked. But he stayed the course as a faithful man who believed in God.

All along the way, there was a calm, steady serenity about my dad. I have to believe it was because he kept God in the picture and did not waver. I am sure his greatest loss was the earlier death of Mom.

I have often written about how impressed I was to hear him pray aloud each morning before breakfast, even when he was alone. Even in his last days, after Dad had pretty well lost his ability to remember things, when I would say a Mass at home with him, he knew the responses to every prayer and responded vigorously. Before he needed nursing care when I would visit him at home, I would sometimes sleep in later than he did, and I would hear him praying the same prayers that he and

Mom and my brother and I said together at the breakfast table. Those kinds of family practices affect us deeply and forever. Dad taught me that keeping in touch with God does not have to be complicated. But it does need to happen faithfully.

The older I get and the more I experience in life, the more grateful I am for the blessings of having such a wonderful family. Mom and Dad were truly my teachers in life and in faith. As I have said before, I believe my parents taught me more by the way they lived than by what they told me.

From Dad I learned the importance—and the value—of work. One summer, Dad got me a job at the Jasper Cabinet Company. He wanted me to experience how many people earn their living. Another summer, I drove a bakery truck. When I think of Dad, I often think of St. Joseph, the husband of Mary and the foster father of Jesus. Blessed John Paul II called St. Joseph *redemptoris custos*, the guardian (or steward) of the redeemer, because of the way in which he cared for the child entrusted to his care.

With Mary, Joseph was privileged to parent Jesus through the early stages of his life. He is a patron for ordinary people trying to become holy in the workaday world.

Based on my dad's example, and with St. Joseph as our patron, I offer four simple considerations about how we can live our call to holiness and place our trust in God in our work at home and elsewhere.

First, make the connection between work during the week and Sunday. Diligence in work is good stewardship.

Ethical practice is good stewardship of work. Work is a way of responding to God's gifts with our God-given talents. If you are disabled by sickness, as I am now, see that as a work of holiness. An intentional awareness of the stewardship of work is a major way in which we can become holy.

Bring your week's work and the fruits of your work as a spiritual offering to the Lord at Sunday Mass. The connection with Sunday Eucharist integrates Christian stewardship of time, talent and treasure with the offering of the Eucharist.

Work is a stewardship offering at Mass on Sunday. What we put in the Sunday offertory collection is an external sharing of the fruit of our daily stewardship of work. The workweek and Sunday are connected.

Secondly, try to seek a right balance of "family love" and "family wealth." Your work or profession is, of course, a significant way in which you exercise your responsibility to provide for your family; or if you are single, it is a way to exercise your responsibility for the welfare of the local community of extended family and friends.

In the pressure of being productive workers, it is difficult to find the right balance. In the world of business, competition in a free market is an ever-present pressure. I encourage spouses to pray for the discernment to make good decisions about how much time should be given to work in order to provide for family, and how much time and energy needs to be spent with family.

Dad and Mom showed us that the priority of family love over family wealth can be lived in a practical way. It's not easy in the climate of secular cultural values that press for material wealth.

Thirdly, try to practice presence of God in your workaday life. A saint of our times, St. Josémaría Escrivá de Balaguer, was a great proponent of the holiness of lay people. He emphasized the notion of what he called "practice of the presence of God."

By this practice, he meant to make us aware of God's presence in our daily work whether at home or away. Believe and be aware that God is with you through the day.

We do that by an occasional short mental prayer such as "Lord, help me;" "Lord, thank you for your help through a tough stretch or the tedium of housework;" or "Holy Spirit, guide me in this next meeting or interview or sale."

Daytime practice of the presence of God will be even more meaningful if we begin with a morning offering, a short prayer of placing the day in God's hands. It is fruitful to spend a few minutes at bedtime reflecting on God's blessings through the day—and also consider whether we acted as if God didn't exist.

When all is said and done, there is no greater resource for God's gift in our lives than the Eucharist on Sunday, or better yet, attending Mass during the week as well. If you want a few minutes of refuge and rest, stop for a visit to a nearby parish church or adoration chapel.

Fourthly, try not to overlook the needy around you. The point Jesus made in the parable of Lazarus and the rich man was not that it is wrong to have wealth. He taught that it is not right to ignore the needs of people around us: material needs, spiritual needs and moral needs, perhaps even in your own home.

The sad thing about the rich man in the parable is the fact that he even knew who Lazarus was, not only that he was in dire straits. Even so, he completely ignored him.

Every one of us has a responsibility in charity to our neighbor. Our responsibility is measured by the blessings that are ours.

These are simple thoughts about the connection of our Christian stewardship at work, at home and in Church. My dad was a practical man, but he showed my brother and me by his example that Christian spirituality doesn't need to be complicated, but it does needs to be intentional.

St. Joseph the Worker, pray for us!

CHAPTER SEVEN

CHARITY

In his great encyclical, *Deus Caritas Est* (God is Love), Pope Benedict XVI writes: "The Church's deepest nature is expressed in her three-fold responsibility: of proclaiming the word of God, celebrating the sacraments and exercising the ministry of charity. These duties presuppose each other and are inseparable. Charity is not a kind of welfare activity that could be left to others, but is an indispensable expression of her very being.

The Church is God's family in the world. In this family no one ought to go without the necessities of life".

The Holy Father reminds us that awareness of this responsibility was evident from the very beginning of the Church. He cites the familiar text from the Acts of the Apostles: "All who believed were together and had all things in common, and they sold their possessions and goods and distributed them to all, as any had need" (Acts 2:44-45). As the Church grew, this radical form of material communion could not in fact be preserved, but its essential core remained: Within the community of believers, there can never be room for poverty that denies anyone what is needed for a dignified life.

I am a great admirer of the fantastic mission of the Missionaries of Charity founded by Blessed Teresa of Calcutta. Their vow to serve the poorest of the poor and to do so cheerfully is based on a single-minded principle. When we reach out to the poor, we not only offer help to the helpless, which is praiseworthy in itself, but Blessed Teresa

taught that when we touch and care for the poor, we touch and care for the very body of Jesus. As our Lord himself said, 'Amen, I say to you, whatever you did for one of these least brothers of mine, you did for me' (Mt 25:40).

I believe that Blessed Teresa is the Saint Francis of Assisi of our times. At the time she celebrated her 82nd birthday, she was recovering from malaria. She also had heart problems, but in spite of her age and infirmities, she prayed that she would live long enough to go to China. After years of refusal, the Chinese government had given her permission to enter that country, where she planned to establish a mission for the helpless poor. By the time of her death five years later in September 1997, Blessed Teresa's sisters numbered nearly 4,000 and were established in 610 foundations in 123 countries of the world, including Hong Kong, China!

In February 2012, Cardinal-elect John Tong Hon asked Catholics in Hong Kong to pray for the intercession of

Blessed Teresa of Calcutta for the restart of China-Vatican dialogue. This came during a Mass to welcome her relic (a drop of her blood on a tiny piece of sack cloth) to Hong Kong. In his homily to about 1,000 Catholics, the bishop of Hong Kong said both Blessed Teresa and Blessed John Paul II, whose relic (a lock of his hair) was interred permanently at the cathedral in November, shared concerns about China. "Mother Teresa not only visited Hong Kong and mainland China, but always wanted to establish her congregation in the mainland," said the cardinal-elect, adding that "her dream was partially fulfilled" with the Missionaries of Charity arriving in the Special Administrative Region [of China] in 1983.

Blessed Teresa of Calcutta is probably best known for her respect for human life. Wherever they are, her Missionaries of Charity not only serve the poorest of the poor, they also witness to the profound dignity of human life.

I came to know and admire Mother Teresa and her Missionaries of Charity personally because she visited Memphis twice while I was bishop there and she founded a mission for homeless and abused women and children in the poorest and most dangerous neighborhood in the community. The sisters in Memphis also opened a safe home for single pregnant women who have no home. More than anything else, they are known to be a haven of prayer and safe cheerful love for people of all walks and strata of life in an otherwise dangerous neighborhood. In prayer and in action, they live respect for human life under most difficult circumstances.

The Missionaries of Charity have no guaranteed income and do not accept a salary or compensation. Yet their food cabinets are full, and they have what they need to serve the poor. They have helped countless women choose life rather than abortion, and many volunteers are strengthened in faith because they have witnessed the sisters serving Jesus in the poorest of the poor.

For the Missionaries of Charity, poverty is real. They carry only one extra religious habit when they move from mission to mission. They sleep on cots and do without television and other amenities of life that we take for granted. Prayer is the center of their day and prayer daily moves them out in pairs and on foot into dangerous neighborhoods looking for the homeless, the uncared for, those deprived of the good news of the Gospel.

They especially look after children and the elderly, the most vulnerable. I can testify, these women religious are the most cheerful and joyful people I have ever met. Do they believe in a consistent ethic of life? You better believe it, but they emphasize prevention of abortion because (as Blessed Teresa used to ask) who else will speak for the 1.6 million helpless and voiceless unborn who are aborted annually? She reminded us that a society that is callous to the most vulnerable and helpless of its members is a society that has lost its soul and is on the brink of unbridled violence.

St. Francis of Assisi was a prophet who spoke for the beauty of life and creation in his day. Blessed Teresa's Missionaries of Charity and countless others do so in our own times.

I thank God for the grace to have met Blessed Teresa of Calcutta. She showed me (and millions of others) what it means to believe that Jesus continues to live among us, especially in the poor and the lonely all around us. Her humility and her humor taught us that there are mature ways to deal with anger about the unfairness of life. Blessed Teresa's life made many of us uneasy because she lived the Gospel and didn't just talk about it. Yet she was never judgmental about those of us who are not so responsive to God's grace.

Blessed Teresa touched my heart with two sayings. The first was, "Bishop, pray that I don't spoil God's work." And, second, as she was leaving Memphis, just before she got on the airplane she said to me, "Bishop, when you put the drop of water in the chalice at Mass, pray that I be dissolved in Christ."

I took her request quite seriously, and ever since I have made her prayers mine.

CHAPTER EIGHT

CATECHISM

In October 1992, Pope John Paul II promulgated the *Catechism of the Catholic Church*. This catechism provides the normative teaching of the Catholic faith, and it represents an invaluable resource for everyone who wants to know what we Catholics believe.

In 1994, an Ad Hoc Committee for the Use of the Catechism was established by the bishops of our country. The major task of this committee was to review religion textbooks with an eye to conformity with the teaching of the new catechism. The review process revealed a pattern of unwitting but considerable deficiencies in textbooks then in use. To some degree, the deficiencies of the textbooks resulted from an overcorrection intended to establish more contemporary teaching methodologies.

In 1997, the Holy See published a revised *General Directory for Catechesis* that focuses on how the faith should be taught as a companion piece to the new catechism. In subsequent years, the bishops of our country published a revised *National Directory for Catechesis*, which seeks to achieve a proper balance between content of faith and how that content is taught. We also published *Our Hearts*

Were Burning Within Us: A Pastoral Plan for Adult Faith Formation in the United States and a United States Catholic Catechism for Adults.

In 1994, I was asked to chair our national bishops' Committee on the Use of the *Catechism of the Catholic Church*. When we began our work, our concern as teachers and pastors was for several generations of children and youth who, for a variety of reasons, didn't get the formation and information about our faith that is needed to understand and live authentically our Catholic way of life. Many are seeking that knowledge now through our adult education programs, and we bishops want to provide catechetical materials and methods of instruction that will meet the challenges of our time.

Before his election as Pope Benedict XVI, then-cardinal Joseph Ratzinger served as prefect of the Congregation for the Doctrine of the Faith. This Vatican congregation is charged with the responsibility to promote the teaching of the Church in its totality and to defend it when perceived necessary.

Cardinal Ratzinger carried out his charge whether it was popular to do so or not. I think people forget that if Church doctrine shifted with the intellectual tides of every age, we would no longer have the Catholic faith and there would be no Catholic Church. Continuity is a key to authenticity.

I am proud to call myself a disciple of Pope Benedict—both now and when he was prefect of the Congregation for the Doctrine of the Faith. By God's grace, he has been a blessing for our Church. He is unrivaled as an astute and balanced theologian. I have little patience with his critics, who often enough have never read his writings. Anyone who reads what Joseph Ratzinger has written—either before or after his election as pope—can see that he is never heavy-handed or rigid, but always speaks the mind of the Church, as he understands it, with a firm but gentle voice.

Pope Benedict is a person who knows how to speak the truth with love. In my dozen or so encounters with him, I found him to be engaging, humble and serene. Several times, I met him on the street on his way to or from a bookstore. He wore a simple black cassock. He stopped to visit for a few minutes, and he had a phenomenal memory for names. In fact, once when our paths crossed, Cardinal Ratzinger smiled, waved his finger at me and said, "Ah, yes, büchlein, büchlein, the little book" which is what my surname (Buechlein) means in German!

While a lover of the tradition and heritage of the Church, Pope Benedict is thoroughly committed to the complete implementation of the teachings of the Second Vatican Council. He knows the origins and development of the council's documents because he was there and had a direct hand in crafting several of them. He is also thoroughly acquainted with the Church Fathers and with the development of the Church's doctrines during the past two millennia.

One time, I asked Pope John Paul II what he thought would be the major accomplishment of his papacy. Without hesitation, he said, "the *Catechism of the Catholic Church*." Cardinal Ratzinger was the major producer of this extraordinary compendium of our faith. He once remarked that initially he wasn't sure that developing a contemporary catechism could be accomplished satisfactorily. He got it done. And what a treasure it is for the Church in our time!

Pope Benedict XVI is a timely international leader to carry forward the new catechism's teaching. This pope is a profound exponent of the complimentarity of faith and reason in a society that wants to relegate God and religion to the private sector as if they are irrelevant to the economic, political and cultural realities of the modern world. He is an ardent champion for the dignity of human life, and he is a sensitive man, who is both sophisticated and simple—a holy, gentle man.

During my work as chairman of the national bishops' committee on the use of the *Catechism of the Catholic Church,* much of our time was spent reviewing textbooks. (I am especially grateful to Msgr. Daniel Kutys who was Executive Director of the USCCB Secretariat of Evangelization and Catechesis during the years that I chaired this important committee.) Over the years we observed a pattern of doctrinal deficiencies among the catechetical series we reviewed. I want to emphasize that these deficiencies were found only in those series that were submitted to us and should not necessarily be generalized to all catechetical materials. While the textbooks we reviewed often treated some doctrinal themes quite well, we noted a trend of doctrinal incompleteness and imprecision. When I reported our findings to the body of bishops at our annual meeting, I pointed out that in many of these textbooks there was:

- insufficient attention to the Trinity and the Trinitarian structure of Catholic beliefs and teachings

Continued on page 68

Carl and Rose Buechlein's wedding photo.

ABOVE
*The Buechlein family
with their dog Jackie.*

LEFT
*Charlie and Mark in
their red wagon.*

LEFT
Mark Buechlein
at age 2 and a half

BELOW
The Buechlein family

Mark with his mother Rose and his brother Charlie on the day of his First Communion.

Mark's eighth grade graduation class, Holy Family School.

ABOVE
*Charlie and Marge
Buechlein on their
wedding day.*

RIGHT
*U.S Marine
Charles Buechlein
and his wife, Marge*

Carl and Rose Buechlein

The Buechlein family home in Jasper, Ind.

RIGHT
Mark Buechlein as a
seminarian at Saint Meinrad.

BELOW
First Mass at Holy
Family Church

First Mass with the family

Mass with theologians

Mass with Archbishop William Borders

ABOVE
Priesthood
Ordination photo

RIGHT
Rector's Report

Teaching Theologians

Bishop Buechlein and his father, Carl

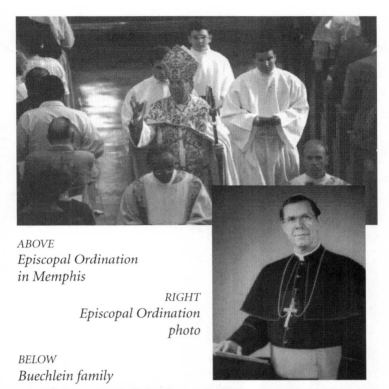

ABOVE
*Episcopal Ordination
in Memphis*

RIGHT
*Episcopal Ordination
photo*

BELOW
Buechlein family

Bishop Buechlein with Mother Teresa in Memphis

25th anniversary of priesthood celebration with Mother Teresa

Bishop Buechlein with Pope John Paul II

Archbishop Buechlein, Pope John Paul II and Archbishop James Keleher

Incensing the altar

Installation as Archbishop of Indianapolis

verwhelmed with the realization that he shares the fullness of the Priesthood of Christ, the bishop envisions his own relationship with his priests after no other pattern than that of the Eternal High Priest with His apostles, as portrayed in the Gospel. It is a humbling responsibility that he shoulders when he becomes the Ordinary of a diocese— +Joseph Cardinal Ritter ·1954

A Bishop and his Priests

Archbishop of Indianapolis Official photo

Archbishop Buechlein greets members of the young Church

LEFT
Pilgrimage
to Assisi

Golden Jubilarians

RIGHT
Official photo

BELOW
Celebrating Mass

Visiting with children at Our Lady of Lourdes School

In the Archbishop's office at the
Archbishop Edward T. O'Meara Catholic Center

More than 30,000 Catholics from central and southern Indiana gathered in Indianapolis for the Great Jubilee on Sept. 16, 2000, to celebrate 2,000 years of Christianity and to thank God for all his blessings. It was the largest gathering of Catholics in the history of the archdiocese and one of the largest Jubilee celebrations in the United States that year.

Archbishop Buechlein greets students at Holy Angels School in Indianapolis.

Celebrating Mass at Saints Peter and Paul Cathedral

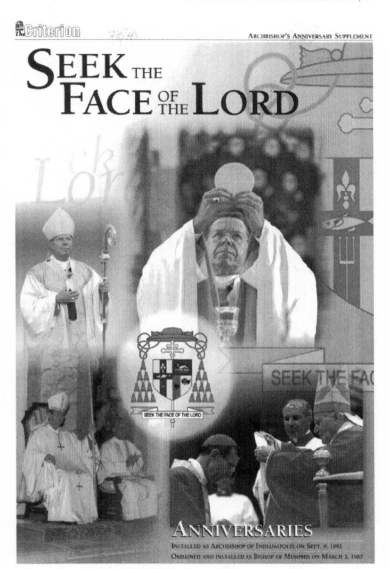

SEEK THE FACE OF THE LORD

ANNIVERSARIES

INSTALLED AS ARCHBISHOP OF INDIANAPOLIS ON SEPT. 9, 1992
ORDAINED AND INSTALLED AS BISHOP OF MEMPHIS ON MARCH 2, 1987

Cover of the Criterion's supplement commemorating the archbishop's 10th anniversary of being a bishop.

Official photo for Jubilee 2000

Archbishop Buechlein with Pope John Paul II

Archbishop Buechlein with Auxiliary Bishop Christopher Coyne

Still seeking the face of the Lord

Archbishop Emeritus Buechlein celebrates 25 years as a bishop

Archbishop Buechlein prays during a 2002 Mass at SS. Peter and Paul Cathedral in Indianapolis honoring his 10th year as archbishop.

Archbishop Buechlein receives his pallium from Pope John Paul II at St. Peter's Basilica at the Vatican on June 29, 1993. The Pallium is a symbol of the fullness of the episcopal office, and is worn by the pope and archbishops.

From left, Father Patrick Beidelman walks beside Archbishop Buechlein during the opening procession of "Celebration in the Spirit of Hope: The Great Jubilee" on Sept. 16, 2000, at the former RCA Dome in Indianapolis. More than 30,000 people worship together at the liturgy, and 3,200 youth and adults were confirmed. Then-seminarian Eric Johnson, right, now a priest and director of the archdiocesan Office of Priestly and Religious Vocations, processes into the RCA Dome behind the archbishop.

Archbishop Buechlein stands with Father Michael O'Mara, left, on June 7, 2006, and comforts mourners after the caskets of six Hispanic homicide victims were carried out of SS. Peter and Paul Cathedral in Indianapolis.

Archbishop Buechlein walks in the 36th annual March for Life on Jan. 22, 2009, in Washington, D.C., with Mary Schaffner, then program coordinator of young adult ministry for the archdiocesan Office of Catholic Education; Servants of the Gospel of Life Sister Diane Carollo, director of the archdiocesan Office of Pro-Life Ministry; and St. Malachy parishioner Donna Johnson of Brownsburg.

The late Lucious Newsom of Indianapolis, left, founder of the Lord's Pantry ministry to the poor, talks with Archbishop Buechlein during a break in the 2004 Archdiocesan Youth Conference on Feb. 29, 2004, at Roncalli High School in Indianapolis.

Pope Benedict XVI speaks with Archbishop Buechlein after the conclusion of the pope's general audience on Oct. 18, 2006, at St. Peter's Square in Rome. A few days earlier, on Oct. 15, 2006, Archbishop Buechlein and the Holy Father concelebrated a canonization Mass during which St. Theodora Guérin, foundress of the Sisters of Providence of Saint Mary-of-the-Woods, was declared a saint.

Above, Archbishop Buechlein answers questions from students during a 2004 visit to Central Catholic School in Indianapolis.

Above, Archbishop Buechlein ritually lays hands on Bishop-designate Paul D. Etienne of Cheyenne, Wyo., during the Dec. 9, 2009, episcopal ordination and installation liturgy at the Cheyenne Civic Center in Cheyenne, Wyo.

Archbishop Buechlein, when he was bishop of Memphis, and the late Blessed Teresa of Kolkata to reporters in Memphis about plans for the Missionaries of Charity to send several sisters to minister to the poor in Memphis.

Above, in a gesture symbolic of his promise of obedience, transitional Deacon Rick Nagel ritually places his hands in the hands of Archbishop Buechlein during a June 2, 2007, ordination Mass at SS. Peter and Paul Cathedral in Indianapolis.

Archbishop Buechlein, center, prays the eucharistic prayer during an Aug. 25, 2010, Mass at St. Roch Church in Indianapolis. Concelebrating the Mass were Father James Wilmoth, left, pastor of St. Roch Parish, and Msgr. Joseph Schaedel, then vicar general.

Right, on Sept. 12, 2005, Archbishop Buechlein, with other officials and the postulator, Andrea Ambrosi of Rome, opens the Cause of Canonization of the Servant of God Simon Bruté, the founding bishop of the Diocese of Vincennes, which became the Archdiocese of Indianapolis.

Venerabili Fratri

Danieli Marco Buechlein, O.S.B.,
Archiepiscopo emerito Indianapolitano, argenteum
consecrationis episcopalis recolenti iubilaeum, faustum
hunc eventum totamque pastoralem navitatem pro spi-
ritali bono fidelium curae eius concreditorum, quam ex-
plevit quaerens faciem Domini (cfr. Ps. 105,4), liben-
ter gratulamur. Ei solacium divinum adprecantes, divi-
nam illam Benedictionem Apostolicam
caelestium gratiarum auspicem, amanter impertimus.

We heartily congratulate our Venerable Brother

Daniel Mark Buechlein, O.S.B.,

Archbishop Emeritus of Indianapolis, as he observes the Silver Jubilee
of his Episcopal consecration.

We are happy with his pastoral assiduity
for the spiritual welfare of the Faithful entrusted to his care,
carried out as he sought the face of the Lord (Ps. 105:4).
We wish him divine solace, and we lovingly bestow on him
our Apostolic Blessing, harbinger of heavenly graces yet to come.

From the Vatican, the eighth day of September in the year 2012.

Benedict XVI

Archbishop Daniel M. Buechlein, O.S.B.
Coat of arms
Definitions explain the parts

- Impalement—The joining of two coats of arms side by side.
- Dexter—The right-hand side of the shield, which is on the viewer's left.
- Sinister—While sinister means "left-handed," on a coat of arms this is the right hand of the viewer. (The right hand of the shield is the left hand of the viewer.)
- Azure in chief—Azure is a name for one shade of the color blue. The word comes from the Old French and Middle English languages.
- Chief—The top of the shield.
- Base—The bottom of the shield.
- Sinister base quarter—The left-hand bottom quarter of the shield.
- Dexter base quarter—The right-hand bottom quarter of the shield.
- Charges—Figures on a colored field.
- External embellishments—Ornamentation surrounding the shield.
- Metropolitan—An archbishop ranking first among the bishops of a province.

- an obscured presentation of the centrality of Christ in salvation history and an insufficient emphasis on the divinity of Christ
- an indistinct treatment of the ecclesial context of Catholic beliefs and magisterial teachings
- an inadequate sense of a distinctively Christian anthropology (that it is precisely in Christ that we have been created in the image and likeness of God)
- an insufficient emphasis on God's initiative in the world with a corresponding overemphasis on human action
- an insufficient recognition of the transforming effects of God's grace
- an inadequate presentation of the sacraments
- a deficiency in the teaching on original sin and sin in general
- a meager exposition of Christian moral life
- an inadequate presentation of eschatology (life after death and the end of time).

In each of these areas of concern the committee presented concrete suggestions to the publishers that made the texts more complete and more faithful to the *Catechism*. The publishers were very cooperative in accepting the recommended and required changes and incorporating them into their texts. This is a great service to our Church and especially to the religion teachers and catechists in our parishes and schools who work so hard to teach our Catholic faith in all its richness and depth.

Proper catechesis helps us live our call to holiness. It is important to keep in the forefront of our minds that everyone who is baptized is called to holiness—a call to be transformed in Christ, to live our faith in service to others and in the acceptance of Christ's way of living until we go home to God.

Catechesis in our schools and in our parishes exists to assist our youth, young adults and adults to live our call to holiness by motivating us to embrace the truth of Christ's revelation and the wisdom of the Church's teaching. A basic knowledge of our faith is a pressing need of every age. I am sorry that some who are parents today did not get that basic knowledge. In our culture, we all need help in facing important questions about our faith and the practices of our Church.

How we provide for this growth in faith is important. No one is helped, especially our youth, if what we believe is perceived simply as a matter of personal choice. Nor do we assist anyone if they are left with the impression that "one church is as good as another."

We are doing better with this now. We have dedicated teachers and catechists. With the help of God's grace, and with resources like the *Catechism of the Catholic Church*, and our national catechetical directory and adult formation guide, we can respond to the challenge given to us by Christ in every age: *Go, therefore, and make disciples of all nations, baptizing them in the name of the Father, and of the Son, and of the holy Spirit, teaching them to observe all that I have commanded you. And behold, I am with you always, until the end of the age* (Mt 28:19-20).

CHAPTER NINE

YOUNG ADULT MINISTRY

Not long after my 25th anniversary of episcopal ordination, I received a visit from a group of young men and women who are part of the Church's growing young adult movement. They were gathered at Saint Meinrad for a mini-retreat, and they stopped by the monastery infirmary to see me. These enthusiastic and faith-filled young adults are students at Indiana University–Purdue University Indianapolis (IUPUI), and they gather regularly at St. John the Evangelist Catholic Church in downtown Indianapolis to pray, learn and share their faith with one another under the vigilant eye of Father Rick Nagel.

The young adult movement is growing in Indianapolis and throughout the world. (I was privileged to attend 3 World Youth Days during my episcopal ministry: Denver and Toronto with Pope John Paul II and Cologne with Pope Benedict XVI.) It is a sign that the Holy Spirit is active in our Church in spite of all the problems we face due to both self-inflicted wounds and the challenges of an increasingly secular world. What a pleasure it is to see happy, well-balanced young women and men who are excited about their faith and who want to be more involved in the Church's ministries of education, health care, social service and witness to the cultural and political changes of our time.

Encounters with young adults like these have been a frequent, joyful occurrence during my 25 years as a bishop (and, of course, of my more than 20 years as a teacher, spiritual director and seminary rector). Vibrant young adults are a sign of life for the Church. They are also our leaders—now and in the future—the clergy, religious and lay leaders who will guide and serve the flock that Christ entrusted to his disciples' care when he returned to his heavenly father.

Ironically, this age group is probably the most neglected when it comes to official Church ministry at the parish and diocesan levels. During my time as a bishop and archbishop, I tried to raise awareness of the importance of young adult ministry—occasionally with great success but more often not as effectively as I had hoped. Something about young adults leads us (bishops, pastors, archdiocesan and parish leaders) to believe that they can take care of themselves while we concentrate on other age groups, especially children. This is a mistake. As I see it, whatever time, effort and money we invest in the young Church comes back to us a thousandfold!

Bishop Simon Bruté College Seminary in Indianapolis is a powerful example of what I mean here. As I write these words, the first transitional deacon from Bruté seminary is preparing for ordination. A year from now, God willing, he will be ordained a priest and others will follow close behind. We wouldn't have this wonderful college seminary, or the "culture of vocation" that it exists to nurture, had it not been for a group of young adults who gathered on the campus of Marian College (now Marian University) on a regular basis to pray together and to live their faith. Their desire for a more intense kind of Christian formation demonstrated to me (and to many others) that there was a need for the kind of house of formation that Bishop Bruté became in its early years. The success of this "experiment" on the Marian campus led directly to the establishment of our "free-standing" college seminary and its formal collaboration with Marian University.

God is smiling on this venture, and we are grateful. In the prayer of dedication, we asked the Lord "that this house may indeed be a school of prayer and a center of divine teaching so that those who come here may discover how God chooses to lead them in service to the Church and the world."

We prayed that "through prayer these young men may be led by your Spirit to seek the way of your truth, that if you are calling them as future ministers of Christ, they will respond with generous hearts and resolute will."

We prayed that "here they will grow accustomed to offering spiritual sacrifices, and by celebrating the liturgy, experience the saving power of the sacraments."

We prayed "that their obedience will lead them to follow the Good Shepherd."

I make a point of the Bishop Bruté College Seminary because, besides the important work of providing a nearby opportunity for young men to see if God calls them to priesthood in a formation program designed for that purpose, we are experiencing another benefit. I believe that the existence of Bishop Bruté College Seminary, to be sure, along with our archdiocesan youth and young adult ministry programs, has enkindled a new "culture of vocation."

What do I mean by a new "culture of vocation"?

Quite simply, I mean that the idea of vocation in general is more noticeably brought to mind for our youth and young adults. I don't mean to suggest that the vocation to priesthood is the only vocation that comes to mind. The fact that many diverse Catholic young men from Bishop Bruté have studied alongside students at Marian University has added the value of encouraging other youth and young adults to wonder what specific plan God might have for them. This creates a culture in which vocations to ordained ministry, to the consecrated life, to marriage and the dedicated single life and to various forms of lay ecclesial ministry and lay witness in the world are seen positively and are nurtured and developed through prayer, sacraments and service on a regular basis as an integral part of the young adults' daily life.

Bishop Bruté College Seminary helps us communicate that baptism initiates everyone on the way of holiness. Every baptized person is called to live a holy life in some specific way. The more common vocation of Catholics is to live the faith as lay persons, whether married or single, and to do so in the stuff of everyday life.

In addition, some of us are called to be holy as consecrated women or men who live a special witness to the Gospel in the Church and the world. Religious sisters, brothers and priests are a unique gift for the life of the Church. And, of course, some of us are called to be ordained deacons, priests or bishops in the ministry of the Church.

The baptismal call to holiness is the foundation of all vocations. For a variety of reasons, awareness of that fundamental call, which is shared by all of us, seems to have been diminished over the years. With that diminishment went the attentiveness to God's call to religious and priestly vocations as well. Why has there been a diminishment in the awareness of vocation in general?

The prevailing values of our culture eclipse the spiritual values that foster vocational alertness. We are, as it were, washed in secular and material values that, in fact, militate against the generous spirit needed for service in the Church and the world. For awhile, not much effort was expended in issuing an invitation to consider the call to holiness in general, and to serve as religious and priests in particular.

Today, many of our youth and young adults are seeking to sidestep excessively materialistic values in search of a deeper meaning in life. Frankly, I find them readily attentive to spiritual direction. With like-minded peers, they signal hope for the future.

They deserve our enthusiastic support!

The young men and women who visited me in the monastery infirmary were full of life. They were excited and grateful that their peers had invited them to become part of the Catholic Association on the IUPUI campus. They thanked me, and their moderator, Father Nagel, for making it possible for them to assume leadership and service responsibilities in our Church.

I was truly inspired—and given hope—by their words and their example. I especially enjoyed the fact that after visiting me they planned to go down by the lake and build a campfire. They are young people having fun, as they should be, while also giving serious consideration to the universal call to holiness and the particular form God's call is taking in their individual lives.

I thought to myself that these young adults are having "holy fun," which is a form of the joy that all of us Christians are called to experience as a result of our liberation from the negative effects of sin and death. I pray that we can give all young people the gifts of happiness, freedom and joy that are our inheritance as children of God!

CHAPTER TEN

CATHOLIC EDUCATION

Since the press conference at which my appointment as archbishop of Indianapolis was announced in July 1992, I have declared myself to be deeply committed to Catholic education. I also declared my deep concern for poor children who deserve the opportunity to break out from the cycle of poverty.

In response to questions from journalists, I said that I would do everything possible to keep our Catholic schools in the center city in Indianapolis and elsewhere alive in the face of the inevitable challenges we would have to face.

The record will show that, in the nearly 20 years since that press conference, our archdiocese has worked very hard to maintain our mission of excellent education and value formation for poor children. Over the years, through the combined generosity of many of our people and corporate and foundation friends, we raised and contributed more than $65 million to the cause of Catholic education, much of it going to poor children in our center-city and rural schools.

Why is Catholic education so important to me?

The founding of our Catholic school "system" had very much to do with the fact that we were an immigrant

Church. It also had to do with maintaining our Catholic faith and culture in a national culture that was predominantly Protestant.

Nor were the circumstances of the day friendly to our ancestors. If the Catholic faith was to be passed on to succeeding generations, our forebears decided that it was necessary to have their own schools in which the faith and our Catholic tradition could be taught to their children.

Traces of that aspect of our Catholic heritage marked my own early years of elementary education. I am pretty sure that is a significant source of my strong convictions about our Catholic schools.

In Dubois County, Ind., where I grew up, there still existed one-room, eight-grade schools during my early childhood. We called them "school houses."

In fact, outside of Jasper (my home town), there had been a Buechlein School near my Grandpa Buechlein's farm. About a mile from my childhood home, there was the Boeckelman School. The names of the schools tell of their German immigrant origin.

My mom's brother, Uncle Adam Blessinger, taught at the Boeckelman School, and there I spent the first two years of grade school. It was kind of like a home school. Most of us children, 25 or so, were cousins, and all of us were Catholic.

An old iron coal stove heated the one room. There was a "recitation bench" at the front of the room where, grade by grade, we would receive and recite the lesson of the day while the other grades worked at their desks or practiced writing on the blackboard.

On Saturday mornings, my brother, Charlie, and I would go to St. Joseph School in Jasper to receive our religious education from Sisters of Providence. I was prepared for first Communion and the sacrament of confirmation on those Saturday mornings.

Our family regularly went to St. Joe's for confession monthly on a Saturday afternoon. That's when the pastor, Msgr. Leonard Wernsing, repeatedly nudged Mom and Dad to transfer Charlie and me to St. Joseph School. I was in the third grade; Charlie was in seventh. That's also where our education came more extensively under the direction and influence of the Sisters of Providence.

St. Joseph School in Jasper opened in 1842; it was the first school founded by Mother Theodore Guérin (now St. Theodora)—another immigrant connection. At the time of my elementary education, some 20 of Mother Theodore's Sisters of Providence were teaching at St. Joe's. Interestingly, at that time, it was also a public school.

Besides receiving an excellent academic education, we also received a solid grounding in our Catholic faith, tradition and culture. I would also add that my vocation to the priesthood found its roots in St. Joe's environment—in addition to my family, of course.

In many ways, my generation of Catholics still experienced somewhat of an immigrant connection in our elementary education. As I look back, I value that historical connection very deeply.

These days, it is not easy to recognize the immigrant context that gave rise to a truly prominent Catholic education system. Many developments account for the loss of that connection, the passing of time and the change in our national culture being major ones. We also regret the loss of the influence of the religious sisters and religious brothers as teachers.

We owe an enormous debt of thanks to those religious who provided so many of us with superb educations and religious formation. They played a momentous role in the historical development of the Catholic Church in the United States.

Now it is only proper to express our gratitude to the lay women and men who have stepped up to take over the important role of teachers and administrators in our Catholic schools. They are doing an excellent job, especially in the face of the challenges of our secular culture.

I have a strong sense of their importance from personal experience. I already mentioned that my Uncle Adam was a lay teacher. My mom was the first lay teacher at Holy Family School (in my home parish) in Jasper in the late 1950s. An aunt also succeeded teaching religious sisters in Dubois County.

Our country's culture is not friendly to some very important values and teachings of our Catholic faith and tradition. And so our Catholic schools continue to be important for handing on the rich heritage we received from our ancestors in the faith. I pray gratefully for our ancestors and all who generously keep the grand tradition of our Catholic schools flourishing!

A fundamental purpose of a Catholic school is to remind our children and youth that their baptism inaugurated for them the call to holiness. The school not only reminds them of the call, but also helps them learn how to live this call in everyday life.

Catechesis in the Catholic faith is at the heart of the evangelizing mission of our schools as it is also the reason for our parish religious education programs. Not only is catechesis intended to provide information to our students, it also proposes gradually to lead children and our youth into a closer relationship with Jesus.

Of course, we are proud of our academic efforts as well. A review of the Indiana Statewide Testing for Educational Progress (ISTEP) scores of our Catholic elementary schools is truly encouraging. But that doesn't tell the whole story of Catholic education. We sometimes speak of the "value-added" features of our educational mission. We not only care about the intellectual development of our students; we help them in the development of their character and overall moral integrity. We care about their physical development and good health. We care about their social development.

The mission of Catholic education comes at a price. Our parishes work hard to make our schools and religious education programs available as widely as possible. Still, in spite of our best efforts to provide tuition assistance, a lot of folks simply can't afford Catholic school tuition. And so our parishes provide solid religious education and faith formation programs to enable our shared call to holiness.

I was away on vacation the day it was announced that Blessed Mother Theodore Guérin would be canonized as a saint of the Church on Oct. 15, 2006. How thrilled the Sisters of Providence at Saint Mary-of-the-Woods and all of us in the archdiocese and throughout Indiana were that wonderful day! As one who has prayed daily to Mother Theodore for years, the news seemed almost too good to be true! Having now witnessed St. Theodora's canonization with my own eyes in the company of so many of her sisters and so many of our priests and lay faithful, and having experienced the unique privilege of concelebrating the canonization Mass with Pope Benedict XVI, I rejoice that one of our own stands proudly among those who have been recognized by the Church for their holiness, their courage and their fidelity to our Lord Jesus Christ!

I have known of the beloved foundress of the Sisters of Providence, St. Theodora (the name under which Mother Theodore Guerin was canonized), since my early grade school days at St. Joseph Parish in Jasper. It is an extraordinary privilege for our archdiocese to have a canonized saint whose body is in a sealed coffin in the Church of the Immaculate Conception at Saint Mary-of-the-Woods, Ind. But it is more than that.

Since the news from Rome, I have done a great deal of reflecting on the meaning of St. Theodora for our local Church in our day and time.

Against all odds, in primitive circumstances, St. Theodora founded schools for poor children because she had a vision of their value both academically and religiously.

Her example gives us pause these days when maintaining excellent Catholic education is so very difficult for our parish communities. Some wonder if we should give up on our mission of Catholic schools, especially in our more challenged parishes.

The courage, valor and generosity of the intrepid St. Theodora are a timely and needed inspiration. I do not believe we could find a more fitting patroness for our challenged apostolate of Catholic schools and Catholic education in general.

One need only read Mother Theodore's accounts of her early missionary activity to sense the struggle that she and her small community experienced in order to find and provide the resources needed to serve Christ's primitive Church in Indiana.

She was a key force in building on the foundation of the Catholic mission valiantly begun by the Servant of God Simon Bruté, our first bishop.

It was difficult enough for the pioneer community of the Sisters of Providence to survive in the austerity of the woods near Terre Haute. Rather than fixing only on their own needs, they ventured to serve God's poor people, especially young women around Indiana.

Sometimes when we worry about the daunting challenges associated with developing and maturing a stewardship way of life for our local Church, St. Theodora provides direction. Her accounts of crossing the often tumultuous Atlantic Ocean in barely seaworthy ships are amazing. Yet, she crossed that stormy ocean several times in order to find resources to carry on Christ's mission in our part of the new world. She summoned the fortitude she needed to overcome her personal fears in order to seek help for the desperate missions in Indiana.

We do not live in the primitive circumstances of the pioneer Sisters of Providence (and other religious foundations) in the 19th century. But we do live in a culture that tends to look away from poverty in our own home missions in Indiana, in other parts of our nation and throughout the world.

I often recall Mother Theodore's words: "But again, I must talk about money. When will the day come that we shall be able to be occupied only with God? Our consolation is that it is for him that we engage in other things."

I pray that under the patronage of St. Theodora

Guérin we will be helped to see beyond the boundaries of our own backyards, so to speak, in order to serve the poor who need the help of all of us.

Mother Theodore had a missionary vision that she pursued, even despite unfortunate opposition from one of the early bishops of Vincennes.

What strikes me is that she held on to that vision of serving the needs of Christ in the wider Church and society while also keeping focused on the needs of her own foundling community of sisters, who lived in poverty both at the Woods and at their earliest missions around Indiana.

When all is said and done, St. Theodora is a model of the centrality of prayer from which all mission flows. She was unswerving in her conviction about the importance of prayer, especially devotion to the Blessed Sacrament and the protection of Our Lady of Providence. The first thing Mother Theodore and her pioneer companions did when they arrived in the Woods was to seek strength and solace before the Blessed Sacrament.

She wrote: "What strength the soul draws from prayer! In the midst of a storm how sweet is the calm it finds in the Heart of Jesus. But what comfort is there for those who do not pray?"

I suggest that we look to St. Theodora for inspiration and courage as we face the never-ending needs of our Church.

From the time I became a bishop, I have been deeply committed to Catholic education and the religious formation of our youths. Our schools and parish catechetical programs are essential to the evangelizing mission of our Church. May they flourish in our time and always!

CHAPTER ELEVEN

MEMPHIS

I have wonderful memories of the five-and-a-half years that I served as bishop of Memphis. These memories come flooding back to me on anniversaries, when I think of certain people, and at unexpected moments for no apparent reason. I'd like to share some of these now—in no particular order, as a kind of stream of consciousness, the way they often occur to me now that I am retired from the daily responsibilities of a bishop.

Monsignor Paul Clunen was a larger than life pastor in Memphis. He welcomed me with open arms and helped me better understand the unique culture and traditions of the Church in West Tennessee. Not every priest was so generous. At my first confirmation as bishop, a priest confronted me in the parking lot and said he didn't think monks should be bishops. He also informed me that he didn't like the man who had been his seminary rector. Fortunately it wasn't me, but I got the message, and at least I knew where I stood!

This priest illustrated something I was told by Ms. Rita Schroeder, a leader in the health care community who at that time was executive director of St. Francis Hospital in

Memphis. She once said, "Bishop, here in West Tennessee, we're 'Baptist Catholics' who are not accustomed to being part of a larger diocese." That helped me see that teaching about the mission of the diocesan Church was a very important part of my responsibility as bishop. Every chance I got, I tried to emphasize that the diocese is all of us—not just the folks who work "downtown" at the chancery.

While I was the bishop of Memphis, I wrote a pastoral letter titled "The Diocesan Church." Because of the particular history of the Church in Tennessee, there was misunderstanding about the meaning of Church. I wrote, "Many still think of 'the Diocese' as that office on Jefferson Avenue somewhere in Memphis. A bureaucratic office is not the Church. A voluntary federation of independent 'corner congregational churches' we are not. *Diocese* is the term the Church gives to a local or 'particular Church.' This means the diocese is not simply a segment of the wider, universal Church, but a concrete realization of it; it is the whole church made visible here and now in this place called West Tennessee. ... The universal Church is the communion of all the local Churches, the dioceses, of the world."

I still remember people in West Tennessee saying to me, "I can see why we need a bishop, but why do we need the diocese? And why do we need a cathedral?" In my pastoral letter I wrote: "The primary unit of the Church is the diocese. The universal Church is the communion of all the local Churches, the dioceses of the world. I am not the bishop of an office or building. Together, all of us, the Catholic bishop, clergy, religious and lay people of West Tennessee are the Catholic Diocese of Memphis. By

God's grace and papal decree we are the People of God made visible as the Apostolic Church here and now in West Tennessee."

My assignment as bishop of Memphis at the age of 48 was the first time in my life that I lived alone. I remember that seemed very strange to me, especially in my early days. My daily prayer helped me remember that I am not really alone at all. Moving from Saint Meinrad after more than 29 years as a monk was disorienting and painful. But as soon as I placed the Blessed Sacrament in the tabernacle of my residence chapel, I felt rooted once more. Christ is with me, and I never have to feel alone.

I think of an elderly African-American woman, now deceased, who was a friend of mine in Memphis. She was an angel of mercy. She was an extraordinary teacher who had to fight her way to get an education because in her day young women, especially young black women, were not supposed to become educated.

"Mama Dora" became a great teacher in the public school system. And when the Church experienced the loss of many religious sisters and brothers as teachers in our Catholic school system, she sacrificed the extra income to teach in Catholic schools, one of the Memphis Diocese's first lay teachers. In retirement, I would say Mama Dora became a preacher. She lectured many of us, lay people and priests, about the Catholic faith and how we should live it. Sometimes she was hard on us, yet we respected her because she cared about our faith. She was a teaching angel of mercy.

When I was consecrated a bishop 25 years ago, I said that my first duty to the folks in the Diocese of Memphis was to be a man of prayer. Many said amen to that. The first ministry of the priest (and bishop) is prayer. Prayer is ministry, and it is pastoral. It is a service that is often hidden and unsung, yet prayer is the hinge of everything else a priest does in service to the people of God.

Bishops and priests do all kinds of things: preaching, teaching, administrating, visiting the sick, helping the poor. But prayer is always the link that holds everything else together. There is a logic and coherence to the life of a priest: As it was for Jesus, celibacy and obedience and a simple way of life threaded together by prayer are the soil in which fruitful priestly ministry thrives.

In the exchange of official documentation at the time of my ordination as a bishop, I was informed that the Holy Father, Pope John Paul II, requested that I emphasize my role as teacher. One of the practical ways I could do that was to teach in the diocesan Catholic weekly newspaper. My regular readers know that I took great pride in the fact that, in my 25 years as a bishop and archbishop, I wrote more than 1,000 newspaper columns. Until my recent illnesses prevented me, I never missed writing my weekly column.

I remember an experience at Memphis Catholic High School in my fourth or fifth year as bishop. I visited one of the junior morality classes and the students' questions surprised me. The first question, a very sensitive one, went something like this: "Do you ever want to quit being a bishop because it's too hard?" My answer was "No, quite the contrary. I have never regretted one day of my life as a priest. It is a wonderful way of life, and it gets better and better. I can't imagine another way of life in which

I could work at the heart of life and reality where I feel I can really make a difference." I also remember saying to the young man, "If you are asking do I ever get frustrated or discouraged? Once in awhile, yes."

A similar question followed from a young woman: "Do you ever doubt your vocation?" No, not for a moment, I said. During seminary is when I had to deal with my doubts. I remember how much I worried and wondered if I could ever speak in public. I wondered if I was a good enough person to be a priest. I pondered about whether or not I wanted to live a celibate life. With the help of God and a lot of good people I made the right decision and now I don't doubt my calling to be a priest, and later, a bishop. And it gets better every year—despite the challenges I have had to face in recent years!

On May 3, 1989, in Memphis, I celebrated my silver anniversary of ordination to the priesthood. Mother Teresa of Calcutta was present because we combined celebrations of the 150th anniversary of the first Mass celebrated in Memphis, the founding of a mission by Mother Teresa and my silver jubilee. I have a card Mother Teresa gave me. She reminded me of the marvelous love Christ has for me and the many blessings I have received in priestly ministry. She also wrote "be humble like Mary and you will be holy like Jesus."

Every year in Memphis there is a candlelight procession attended by thousands of people from around the world in memory of Elvis Presley. It reminds me of the candlelight procession of thousands of people, many of them in wheel chairs or walking with canes, which takes place every night of the year at the shrine of Our Lady of Lourdes in the foothills of the Pyrenees Mountains in southern France. I can't help but mark the contrast between the two rituals—one secular and one sacred. The candles, the slow marching, the quiet demeanor of the participants in the processions are similar features. The focus or purpose of the vigils is somewhat similar, namely to remember a human person. But any other semblance of similarity ends there!

The pronunciation of my family name doesn't sound the way it looks. When I went to Memphis to become the bishop there, the wrong pronunciation was given to the news media. For months, whenever I would give the correct pronunciation I would be told, "That can't be right ... the news anchor of Channel 5 told us how to pronounce it." I learned early on that there is a tendency to take reporting on TV or in the newspaper as gospel. I worry about this because many (not all) reporters put a spin on the news. When it comes to the news media today (and all the scandals that are reported for better or worse) I am reminded of a saying one of my classmates used to quote (from his grandmother): "You always have to tell the truth, but you don't always have to *tell* the truth."

One of my best friends and co-workers during what I like to call my "short stop in Memphis" was J. Peter Sartain, now archbishop of Seattle. There are many, many things I could say about then-Father Sartain's ministry to the People of God in West Tennessee (not to mention his later service as a bishop first in Little Rock, Ark., then in Joliet, Ill., and now in Western Washington state), but I will limit my recollections to remarks he made while serving as vicar general of the Diocese of Memphis.

His topic was the news media's (and our society's) fascination with sensational stories of shattered lives. Father Sartain wrote: "Criminals and victims of their crimes, hurting parents of errant children, the emotionally disturbed with their bizarre behavior, churches and their fragile ministers—all are our sisters and brothers, not objects of our scrutiny. Shattered lives—ours and others'—deserve compassion, not invasion. Each time I let myself be entertained by the hurts of others, I implicitly make objects of those persons, distance myself from them, and thereby beg for more. This is alienation at its most basic. It is the root of indifference and prejudices. We are capable of better."

Father Sartain also wrote: "Priests, ministers, and rabbis bear the awesome calling to speak God's word. Sometimes we preach it well, sometimes badly. Sometimes we live it well, sometimes badly. Yet what sustains our calling, despite the poor mess we make of things at times, is a belief that God does not treat any human person as an object. Let there be no mistake: God is not soft on evil, nor should we be. But neither does God distance himself from us, alienate himself from us, or make us the subjects of his entertainment. Those are human pastimes. God loves us saints and sinners alike. ... There is nothing more purifying than the wrath of God's love. ... It seems to me that in their approach to matters of faith, some members of the media are the last to discover that sin exists. There is something inherently naïve about one who sensationalizes human frailty; he or she misses the point! Believers have always known beyond a doubt that sin exists, that in fact all of us are prone to fall and often do. ... Certainly there is much in religion that is newsworthy, and not all news about religion is comfortable to the believer. Whatever the news about their faith, believers deserve a serious, not a sensational, account of the pertinent issues."

I couldn't say it better. Someday an accurate account of history will note that our Church, under the leadership of its bishops, was among the first to address the complex illness of sexual abuse in our society. Certainly Archbishop Sartain is a powerful example of courageous and faith-filled leadership. As a priest and as a bishop, he speaks the truth with compassion and with integrity—in Jesus' name!

When I received the call from the apostolic pro-nuncio on January 14, 1987, telling me that Pope John Paul II wanted me to be ordained as the third bishop of the Diocese of Memphis, I was stunned. I will never forget that phone call. The pro-nuncio emphasized that the Holy Father had transferred my Benedictine vow of obedience from the archabbot to himself and that he was sure I would obey.

The first opportunity I had, I asked the Holy Father why he asked Benedictine monks to become bishops. He responded with one of his simple one-liners: "Benedictine spirituality has much to offer."

It was a dramatic (and I don't mind admitting, difficult) obedience that moved me from Saint Meinrad Archabbey to Memphis. I relearned the spiritual lesson that obedience to the surprises God gives us brings peace and happiness. After five quick years, I got another phone call from the papal pro-nuncio and another obedience. I felt I had just settled into West Tennessee, but I was to return to Indiana. I love the people of West Tennessee—just as I love my Hoosier brothers and sisters here in Indiana!

One who joins a monastery doesn't expect dramatic vocational changes! Yet the move to Indianapolis reminded me that once more obedience brings many blessings. I had an even more dramatic call to obedience the day my stroke changed my life forever. I have been surprised by grace many times during the past 25 years, but every time God has given me the strength required to say "yes" to his will for me no matter how difficult.

The Diocese of Memphis (the Church in West Tennessee) will always have a special place in my heart. I treasure the wonderful people I worked with there—at the chancery, in our parishes and schools, and in the broader community.

Twenty-five years ago on March 2, 1987, I was ordained a bishop in Memphis. Recently someone asked me about my thoughts after 25 years as a bishop. I admit that in many ways it seems unreal to me still. When I entered the monastic novitiate in 1958, future ordination as a bishop was the farthest thing from my mind. I was just hoping I would know if I should be a Benedictine monk and, later, a priest for the monastic community.

The call 29 years later and the move to West Tennessee came as a shock. The monastic and seminary prayer schedule and practices and readily available spiritual directors and confessors had been a tremendous gift. It was a big change to move to the bishop's residence on busy Poplar Avenue in Memphis. I have learned a lot since then.

CHAPTER TWELVE

HOPE

Our Church teaches that the two greatest obstacles to practicing successfully the theological virtue of hope are presumption and despair. We are guilty of presumption when we convince ourselves that we don't need the grace of Christ, that we can reach our life's goal all by ourselves. The sin of despair leads us in the opposite direction; it persuades us that our efforts are hopeless, that we will never reach our goal no matter what. Christ assures us that if we follow him, and walk in his light, we will not give in to the false hope of presumption or to the darkness of despair.

When I was a young man—healthy and full of energy, I was tempted to think that I could accomplish my life's goals all by myself. Prayer, reception of the sacraments (especially penance), spiritual direction and the constructive criticism I received from family members and good friends helped me keep my ego in check and remember that I can do nothing (nothing at all!) without Christ's grace.

Now that I am older and have experienced serious health problems, my temptation is frequently to despair.

Intellectually I know better, but my emotions often get the better of me, and I worry that I am "damaged goods" or that I have no future and, therefore, no hope. Once again, the tools I need to correct these false perceptions about who I am and what my future is are all around me—gifts that our Church gives to those who search for hope in Christ, the only hope that lasts. Added to the things I mentioned above is the beautiful sacrament of the sick which brings Christ's powerful healing ministry to those of us who are blessed to receive it.

Pope Benedict XVI obviously embraces the Christian virtue of hope. In 2007, he composed the encyclical "*Spe Salvi*" ("Saved by Hope"). The encyclical's title is taken from St. Paul's letter to the Romans: "In hope, we were saved" (Rom 8:24). In this chapter, I'd like to offer some serious reflections on the theological virtue of hope using the Holy Father's powerful teaching on this increasingly important topic for individuals like me who are tempted to lose hope and for our society as a whole .

In his introduction, the pope writes: "According to the Christian faith, 'redemption'—salvation—is not simply a given. Redemption is offered to us in the sense that we have been given hope, trustworthy hope, by virtue of which we can face our present: the present, even if it is arduous, can be lived and accepted if it leads us towards a goal, if we can be sure of this goal, and if this goal is great enough to justify the effort of the journey" (#1).

These words mean a lot more to me now than they did when I first read them. What is it that allows me to "face my present" and to "justify the effort" of my life's journey? The simple answer is Christ. His love for me, and for all humankind; the suffering he endured for my sins and for the sins of all; and the victory he won over the power of death (including my death) with its ominous threat that human life (my life) will end in emptiness and futility. Christ is the source of my hope. I believe this, and I pray for the grace to live it daily.

A natural hope is a poignant yearning of all peoples in our day. In modern culture, there is a heaviness of spirit that is an effect of lowering the bar when it comes to societal values. Materialism, secularism and untoward individualism do not lift the human spirit. In fact, superficial values that ignore the needs of our spiritual soul lead to a deeper natural longing for something better. There is hope for something better in life.

But there is a difference between natural hope and supernatural hope. There is a difference between the natural desire for happiness and a natural confidence in God. We have a natural hope when we plant a seedling that some day it will become a large tree. When we set out on a journey, we have a natural hope that we will reach our destination.

Our Christian hope is far superior to natural hope. Our Christian journey of hope is headed toward the kingdom of eternal life, to supernatural happiness. Our goal is union with God our Father. Christ is the way, the truth and the life. In other words, Christ is our hope.

What natural hope and supernatural hope have in common is a lack of certainty that we will arrive at our goal. Hope is confidence in the unseen. Hope implies a foundation of faith, or trust, in the natural order. The nature of supernatural faith differentiates Christian hope from the natural order. Christ makes all the difference.

Pope Benedict tells us that a distinguishing mark of Christians is the fact that we have a future. We don't know the details of what awaits us after death, but we are certain that our lives "will not end in emptiness" (#2).

What is the source of our hope? In baptism, we received "the full assurance of faith" (Heb 10:22). By the grace of the Holy Spirit, we accepted the gift of unwavering confidence in God's love for us. This is the source of our hope: that God knows us and loves us and that he wants us to be happy with him in this life and in the world to come.

There is no lasting hope anywhere else. If we place our hope in material things, in political systems, in charismatic leaders or in our own abilities, we will always be disappointed. God alone justifies absolute confidence and trust. As Pope Benedict says, "to come to know God—the true God—means to receive hope" (#3).

Because we hope in God, we can live well. Hope does not remove life's difficulties; it allows us to endure them. Hope does not prevent us from sinning, from turning away from God. But supernatural hope allows us to see beyond our own sinfulness to the mercy of God. It allows us to seek forgiveness and to begin again.

To know God is to understand that we have been created by a person who loves each one of us individually and who invites us to share his life fully. We are not the random result of some evolutionary accident. We are the family of God, and we have a future filled with hope.

To know God is to experience his divine love and to receive his promise of happiness now and in the life to come. As Pope Benedict says, "The dark door of time and the future has been thrown open. The one who has hope lives differently; the one who hopes has been granted the gift of new life" (#2).

With this wonderful gift of hope comes an awesome responsibility. As best we can, we must reject the darkness of sin and death, and live in the light. And we must be evangelizers—people who proclaim and live the Gospel of Jesus Christ. We are to share our hope with others.

The Gospel "makes things happen and is life-changing," Pope Benedict tells us. (#2). Hope in Christ calls us to conversion. It invites and challenges us to accept Christ's life-changing love. Because we hope in Christ, we are free to choose life. And once we make this choice, and renew it daily through prayer and the sacraments, we can come to know him, love him and serve him. To know God in Christ means to receive hope.

Pope Benedict describes three essential "settings" for our search for God, and for learning and practicing hope.

The first setting is prayer, which the Holy Father calls a "School of Hope." Prayer opens our hearts to God. It stretches us—challenging us to move beyond our own preoccupations and desires. "When we pray properly, we undergo a process of inner purification which opens us up to God and thus to our fellow human beings as well" (#33).

Christian prayer is always personal, an encounter between each individual and God. But prayer is never individualistic. As the pope teaches, even personal prayer "must be constantly guided and enlightened by the great prayers of the Church and of the saints, by liturgical prayer, in which the Lord teaches us again and again how to pray properly" (#34).

In prayer, we speak to God and he speaks to us. We become open to God, and he directs us away from our self-centeredness to the service of others. This is how prayer teaches us to hope—by reminding us that we are never alone and by placing us in the presence of God, the true source of our hope.

God is the foundation of hope. In prayer, we find hope in "the God who has a human face and who has loved us to the end, each one of us and humanity in its entirety. His kingdom is not an imaginary hereafter situated in a future that will never arrive; his kingdom is present wherever he is loved and his love reaches us" (#31).

The second essential setting for learning and practicing hope is action.

Pope Benedict tells us that "all serious and upright human conduct is hope in action" (#35). This is why we get out of bed in the morning—because we believe that our efforts, our work and our relationships can make a difference. Certainly, we encounter obstacles in our daily life, failures and disappointments that tempt us to wonder whether we can really make a difference after all. Living in the monastery infirmary—in spite of all the wonderful care I receive—I often wonder what difference I am making now and what (if anything) can I expect to accomplish in the future. The temptation is not to get out of bed each day, but that would be a sin against hope.

Christian hope remains steadfast even in the face of personal failures and the failures of humanity. Ours is a lasting hope. We know we cannot build the kingdom of God by our own efforts alone, and we know that the mission we have been given—as individuals and as

Church—will not be a finished product until the Lord comes again. In the meantime, we keep working; we do not lose hope. No matter where we are or what our situation is!

Pope Benedict writes, "It is important to know that I can always continue to hope even if in my own life, or in the historical period in which I am living, there seems to be nothing left to hope for" (#35). Why do we remain hopeful in the face of seemingly hopeless challenges and insurmountable evil? Because we have faith in God who loved us so much that he sent his only son to redeem us. Because, with St. Paul, we believe that "neither death, nor life, nor angels, nor principalities, nor things present, nor things to come, nor powers, nor height, nor depth, nor anything else in all creation, will be able to separate us from the love of God in Christ Jesus our Lord" (Rom 8:38-39).

The third essential setting for learning and practicing hope is suffering. This is the ultimate test—how we handle the mystery of suffering. As individuals, and as a society, we are challenged to accept (and not to avoid or deny) the fact that suffering is an inescapable part of human life.

We Christians can accept suffering, and not run away from it, because Christ freely chose to suffer for us and with us. We can join our suffering with his and, so, be witnesses (martyrs) who choose to sacrifice our comfort and security for the sake of the Gospel.

Prayer, action and suffering are "schools of hope." We pray that the Holy Spirit will sustain us in our efforts to learn, and to practice, this great Christian virtue of hope.

As Pope Benedict reminds us: "Life is a voyage on the sea of history, often dark and stormy, a voyage in which we watch for the stars that indicate the route. The true stars of our life are the people who have lived good lives. They are lights of hope. Certainly, Jesus Christ is the true light, the sun that has risen above all the shadows of history. But to reach him, we also need lights close by—people who shine with his light and so guide us along our way" (#49). I often reflect now on the people who were most instrumental in my life—as a child, as a young monk and priest and as a bishop. They were stars—beacons of light—who guided me in my life's journey.

Of course, the greatest witness to hope is Mary, Star of Hope, whose every word and action points the way to Jesus, her son. "With her yes," the Holy Father writes, "she opened the door of our world to God himself; she became the living ark of the covenant in whom God took flesh, became one of us and pitched his tent among us (cf Jn 1:14)" (#49).

We look to Mary because she experienced the confusion and anxiety that we do. She had reason to despair because of the "sword of sorrow" that pierced her heart. But Mary never gave up hope. It sustained her all the way to the foot of the cross and to the joy of her son's resurrection and the coming of the Holy Spirit at Pentecost. Pope Benedict tells us that Mary's hope made her "the image of the Church to come which carried the hope of the world in her womb across the mountains of history" (#50).

Every significant stage in Mary's life—from the moment she was visited by the archangel Gabriel and learned that she was to become the mother of her Lord, through the disappointments of his public ministry, until she stood beneath the cross—she was repeatedly confronted with choices that required blind faith in God's Providence.

From a human perspective, Mary had every reason to be afraid and anxious. In every case, Mary said yes to God's will. She chose to trust in divine Providence. She gave witness to the hope that depends totally on God's loving care. Mary accepted many things that she did not understand, and she placed her hope in the only thing that is always trustworthy: the love and fidelity of the Triune God.

As I reflect on the theological virtue of hope, at a time in my life when hope can be hard to hold onto on a day-to-day basis, I pray more fervently than ever before:

> O Mother of Holy Hope, show me (and all your children) the way to Jesus, your son. Bless us all as we continue the journey of hope in Christ that was begun at the time of our baptisms and sustain us by your powerful intercession as we pass through this valley of tears to the place of lasting joy prepared for each of us by Christ.

> Together with St. Theodora Guérin, Servant of God Simon Bruté, St. Francis Xavier and all the saints, show us the way to Christ our Hope so that, like you, we may say "yes" to God's will and be witnesses to hope—now and always! Amen.

CHAPTER THIRTEEN

MENTORS

In the preceding chapter, I quoted the following statement from Pope Benedict XVI's 2007 encyclical, "*Spe Salvi*" ("Saved by Hope"):

"Life is a voyage on the sea of history, often dark and stormy, a voyage in which we watch for the stars that indicate the route. The true stars of our life are the people who have lived good lives. They are lights of hope. Certainly, Jesus Christ is the true light, the sun that has risen above all the shadows of history. But to reach him, we also need lights close by—people who shine with his light and so guide us along our way" (#49).

I then commented that I often reflect now on the people who were most instrumental in my life—as a child, as a young monk and priest and as a bishop. I believe that they were stars, in Pope Benedict's use of the term—beacons of light—who guided me in my life's journey. I'd like to take a moment now to name some (certainly not all) of the people who influenced me profoundly over the years and to say a word or two about how I remember them now.

Family is the first great influence on those of us who are privileged to have parents who love us, nurture us and teach us what life is all about. I've already mentioned my parents, Carl and Rose Buechlein. Dad was always a strong, quiet presence in my life. Mom was a source of practical wisdom. Together they formed me and gave me the gift of their strong faith. My brother, Charlie, deserves a place of honor in my list of mentors. He inherited Mom's common sense and Dad's steadfastness in tough times. His wife, Marge, is also one of my heroes. I call her "a trooper in tragedy" because of her ability to bear sorrow with dignity and hope while sustaining the rest of her family along the way. My nephews and nieces can be characterized as follows: Mark is strong but silent; Michael is "an idea guy;" John is an attentive father; Grace is a gift to people "on the margins;" and Anne has always been a strong support to me, a familiar face at archdiocesan events.

My monastic family also contains many "stars" who helped me see the way to Christ. Father Herman Ramoser was a holy man and a gentle-but-firm administrator who served as rector of the minor seminary at Saint Meinrad for many years. All who knew him respected and loved him, and his influence on me was very deep. Archabbot Gabriel Verkamp was a tremendous support to me when I served as president-rector of the School of Theology. He had a no-nonsense way of assessing people. (He once said, "A young monk either has sense or he doesn't.") And he was willing to take risks, even in situations that he didn't fully understand, so long as he trusted the people involved. Father Gregory Chamberlin was my good friend and classmate. He has the biggest heart of anyone I have ever known. Father Aelred Cody was a vigilant confrère and mentor during cloudy days when I studied at Sant'Anselmo in Rome. Father Hilary Ottensmeyer was another source of inspiration. He taught me how to form, and then lead, a team of administrators and to collaborate (and delegate) rather than micromanage. Archabbot Timothy Sweeney and I worked closely together during my years as president-rector. He was responsible for Saint Meinrad's new monastery and library and for a substantial renovation of the Archabbey Church. Archabbot Timothy was not particularly happy when Pope John Paul II called me to be Bishop of Memphis, but as a faithful man of the Church he accepted it and did everything he could to help me make the transition from monastic life to episcopal ministry. His successor, Archabbot Lambert Reilly was a great support to me as archbishop of Indianapolis by his prayers and frequent correspondence. Archabbot Justin Duvall, Saint Meinrad's current archabbot, is a serene leader following in the footsteps of many great men who have led our community since its founding in 1854. I admire him, and I'm grateful to him for his witness as a spiritual father.

Marilyn Brahm was my administrative assistant at Saint Meinrad. She was an anchor who kept my feet on the ground and helped me put order and discipline into the often chaotic daily life of a seminary rector! Msgr. Jerome Neufelder, a priest of the Diocese of Evansville who served as Spiritual Director in the School of Theology, was a good friend and a strong support to me as a new seminary rector. John S. MacCauley was Saint Meinrad's first director of development. John taught me his distinctive "philosophy of development," which emphasized vision and values over finances and fundraising. The lessons I learned from John MacCauley were invaluable during my years as president-rector, bishop and archbishop. When I was able to share with people of faith my vision for the future (the Church's vision!) and invite them to share generously their God-given gifts of time, talent and treasure, they responded wholeheartedly. My friend Dan Conway was the premier disciple of John MacCauley. Dan has been a great help to me over the years, including in the preparation of this book of reflections.

My responsibilities as president-rector brought me into contact with many bishops. Indianapolis Archbishop George J. Biskup was a real father to me. His successor, Archbishop Edward T. O'Meara was a true friend "to the end." I was privileged to know Cardinal John O'Connor of New York who asked my opinion on a wide range of issues facing priests and seminary leaders today. I have been privileged to work closely with many bishops, including all the bishops in Indiana (especially my good friend Bishop Charles Thompson) and Cardinals Francis George, Donald Wuerl and Timothy Dolan, and I have come to admire them for their dedication to the mission of our Church. In an earlier chapter, I spoke of my deep appreciation and respect for Cardinal Joseph Ratzinger, our present pope. Blessed John Paul II and his successor, Pope Benedict XVI, both had a profound influence on me especially during my early years as a bishop.

In my chapter on the Diocese of Memphis, I mentioned two extraordinary pastors—Msgr. Paul Clunen, a model of loyalty and love for the Church, and Father J. Peter Sartain (now the archbishop of Seattle). Msgr. Clunen was a distinguished southern gentleman in the best possible sense of that term. Then-Father Sartain was an eloquent teacher of the faith who was not afraid of tough topics and who was able to lead our people calmly through many storms. (I believe this is why the Holy See chose Archbishop Sartain for the very difficult assignment of apostolic delegate to the Leadership Conference of Women Religious).

My years as archbishop of Indianapolis brought me into close contact with many outstanding priests, religious and lay people. There is no way I can name them all! Msgr. Joseph Schaedel served as vicar general for most of my time in Indianapolis. I could always count on him to take my place when necessary and to do so with a ready wit! Suzanne Yakimchick and, later Annette (Mickey) Lentz served with me in the role of chancellor. Suzanne also directed our pastoral ministries. Her care for women and men abused by archdiocesan personnel was extraordinary. Mickey led our education ministries for many years. A dedicated teacher, principal and archdiocesan leader, Mickey was steadfast and loyal—and always with a smile on her face!

All of the women and men who served on the archdiocese's Management Council during my time as archbishop were an inspiration to me. (As I write these words, I think of Bill Bruns, Charlie Gardner, Dan Elsener, Jeff Stumpf, Mike Halloran, Joe Therber, David Milroy, Greg Otolski, David Siler, Msgr. Bill Stumpf, Msgr. Fred Easton, Msgr. Paul Koetter, Fathers Steve Giannini and Jerry Kirkhoff and many more.) I did my best to choose good, talented and loyal people to provide leadership for archdiocesan ministries. I gave them clear direction. Then I trusted them to do their jobs without interference from me. Ford Cox was my executive assistant for many years. He was loyal and efficient—especially in tough times.

Then, of course, I call to mind all the priests who collaborated with me in Memphis and Indianapolis. (Father Rick Nagel, who stepped up to offer me daily pastoral care after my stroke, comes to mind. As pastor of St. John the Evangelist, the downtown parish in Indianapolis, he put a smile on the face of the Church during Super Bowl Sunday!) No bishop can succeed in his pastoral mission without the help of faithful, hard-working priests. I had more than my share of outstanding brother priests, and in both dioceses, it was always my special joy to get to know our seminarians personally and to assist in their priestly formation. Ordination Day is a special day for every bishop, but I took particular pride in ordaining deacons and priests for service to the Church in West Tennessee and Central and Southern Indiana. It's one of the things I miss most now that I am an emeritus archbishop!

The final group of inspiring people that I want to acknowledge are the caregivers in Indianapolis and at Saint Meinrad who have done so much for me during my various illnesses over the past few years. They have truly gone the extra mile in their professional, and very personal, service to me. I have not always been the best patient, but the women and men who cared for me during some very difficult moments in my life have truly been witnesses to the healing ministry of Jesus. I am deeply grateful.

Did I miss anyone? Without question. So many people have influenced me during the past 74 years of my life that it would be impossible to name them all. Dear family members, confrères, friends and co-workers, you know who you are. Please accept my heartfelt appreciation and thanks for all that you have shared with me over the years.

I'd like to conclude this chapter where I began—by recalling Pope Benedict's powerful image of life as "a voyage on the sea of history, often dark and stormy, a voyage in which we watch for the stars that indicate the route." The Holy Father reminds us that "the true stars of our life are the people who have lived good lives. They are lights of hope." These are the people in our lives who shine with the light of Christ and so guide us along our way to him.

The people identified in this chapter, and many more like them, have guided me on my life's journey. I thank God for them every day, and I pray that I may be worthy of their trust.

CHAPTER FOURTEEN

SAINT MEINRAD

*O*ra et labora (prayer and work) is a Benedictine motto. The life of a monk is designed to achieve a balance between these two fundamental human activities. In his Holy Rule, which describes the pattern of life that monks should follow, St. Benedict describes the monastic life as "a school of the Lord's service." A monastery is much more than a building or a residence for monks. It is a place where monks pray together, learn together and work together in order to live the Christian life according to

Saint Meinrad Archabbey

their particular vocation.

I entered the monastery at Saint Meinrad in July 1958 when I was 20 years old. Benedictines from Saint Meinrad had served at St. Joseph Church in Jasper, Ind., where my brother and I received our formal religious instruction from our pastors and from the Sisters of Providence. I went to the minor seminary at Saint Meinrad to discern my vocation. Six years later, after much prayer and counseling from the Fathers who taught me and served as spiritual guides, I answered the call to monastic life at Saint Meinrad and entered the novitiate. A few years later, I made my solemn profession of vows on August 15, 1963. Shortly afterward, on May 3, 1964, I was ordained a priest for the monastic community and began what would eventually be 23 years of service to the Church in St. Meinrad's seminary apostolate before Pope John Paul II called me to episcopal ministry and transferred my vow of obedience directly to himself and his successors in the See of Peter.

As my archbishop predecessors have testified before me, I can say quite objectively that Saint Meinrad Archabbey and Seminary are a special treasure of the Archdiocese of Indianapolis and the Universal Church. Since 1854, Benedictine monks, originally from Switzerland, have been praying the Liturgy of the Hours and celebrating Mass several times a day, every day without interruption. Even on the day the monastery burned down in September 1887, the monks continued to pray the daily office.

Think about it. Every day for 158 years the monks have prayed with and for the Church several times a day, no matter what was happening in our world. They did so on the day of the Great Fire, they did so through the world wars and the Great Depression; they did so on the day when a man first stepped onto the moon and on other historic days like those tragic ones of the assassination of President John F. Kennedy and Dr. Martin Luther King, Jr., or the attempted assassination of Pope John Paul II; no matter what has happened or is happening in this world of ours, monks went to church to pray and that is what they continue to do today. As one of them, I am proud of that history, and with them I am grateful for God's blessing on the monastic community over these many years.

Think of what a powerhouse of prayer Saint Meinrad Archabbey is for our Church. Isn't it a tremendous witness that some people in this world are so convinced of God's love that they will commit their lives to pray day in and day out as their primary work (the "Work of God" as Saint Benedict calls it)? Nothing else takes precedence. Is there any more powerful witness that we human persons need God and that there is a kingdom coming where, finally, "every tear will be wiped away"? Now more than ever before, our world, our society, our human family—indeed our Church—need to be reminded that we need God.

Saint Meinrad also offers something quite unique and quite challenging. Since 1862, the Benedictine monks have prepared candidates for the priesthood. The seminary has been a tremendous blessing for our archdiocese and, in fact, for the Church in the United States and many other countries as well. Most of the priests of Indiana were educated under the direction of the monks at Saint Meinrad. Most of our current graduate-level seminarians are being educated and given a spiritual and pastoral formation on a campus where there is daily, uninterrupted, faithful prayer. Anyone who lives at (or visits) Saint Meinrad is touched by the sense that there is more to life and reality than meets the eye. Yes, we need God and we need reminders like the "holy hill."

What did I learn in the "school of the Lord's service" that is Saint Meinrad Archabbey? I learned many things from the formal education and monastic formation I received at Saint Meinrad, but I also learned a great deal from the personal witness and fidelity to Benedictine spirituality of my confrères, my brothers in monastic life. I believe all the things they taught me—by their words and their example—can be summarized using the Benedictine motto, *ora et labora* (prayer and work).

At Saint Meinrad, I developed, and deepened, the practice of prayer given to me by my parents and by my pastors and elementary school teachers at St. Joseph Parish. I also learned to take the hands-on work experience my father made sure I had before I entered the monastery and apply it to Saint Meinrad's primary apostolic work, the education of priests for the Church.

I talk and write a lot about prayer, and I have done so for the 25 years that I have been a bishop and for 23 years before that as a priest. One of my reasons for gratitude when I was ordained a bishop in Memphis was that my monastic formation at Saint Meinrad had schooled me in the habit of praying. To be a man of prayer—first and foremost—was a top priority in my ministry as bishop and archbishop, and it is especially important now that I am an "emeritus" archbishop with no administrative responsibilities.

As a baptized Christian, a monk, a priest and a bishop, I am called to develop an intimate personal relationship with Jesus Christ. With the help of many others (including my parents and family, my friends and co-workers in monastic life and in pastoral ministry, and the Catholic faithful in the Diocese of Memphis and Archdiocese of Indianapolis), I have learned to place prayer first and foremost in my life.

While a young seminarian and monk at Saint Meinrad, I prayed to the Blessed Virgin Mary every night, most often before her shrine as Our Lady of Einsiedeln in the archabbey church. Her unfailing protection continues. Needless to say, there are many things I could say about Blessed Mother Mary. Her protection of my vocation goes back many, many years. Her intercession, and her loving care, are more important to me now than ever.

One of the positive consequences of my cancer and subsequent stroke is the impetus to spend more time praying for others who are stroke victims, have cancer or any other debilitating illness. During chemotherapy, I learned to sit patiently and pray. Anyone who has been sick and waits for a doctor's appointment or lies on a gurney waiting for a scan of some kind knows exactly what I mean. I especially notice how much poor people have to wait for even the most basic needs of their lives.

I wonder now about how some of my fellow patients are doing. I know some have gone home to God. But I run into companion lymphoma survivors like Rob, who had to go to work even while undergoing the difficulties related to chemotherapy. I remember a seminarian, Dominic, who while undergoing chemotherapy continued his formation for the priesthood at Saint Meinrad. There are many such stories. I still undergo periodic scans and blood tests to check things out. I can't help but wonder each time if I am going to get a good report. Some folks don't. But I continue with my first reaction to the diagnosis of cancer back in 2008 and to my stroke three years later: God's will be done.

I think of my doctors, nurses and health care providers. They have a very special mission, and are great people in my book. They deserve the support of our prayer and gratitude. I guess I will always pray for a deeper understanding of the meaning of my having had serious illnesses. I know God does not want bad things to happen to us. But he permits it. Since original sin some things go wrong simply because they can. But it is important to see them as opportunities to join our suffering to those of Christ.

I'm glad I learned to deepen my ability to pray at Saint Meinrad. It certainly has sustained me during more than 50 years of monastic life, priesthood and episcopal ministry. To pray with the Church, in intimate communion with Jesus Christ, helps make life worthwhile no matter how dark and gloomy things may look at times.

Monks consider prayer (the work of God) to be our first priority, but St. Benedict urges his monks to devote themselves to worthwhile work. Throughout the more than 1,500 years since Benedict wrote his Holy Rule, monks have engaged in many different kinds of work including manual labor, farming, teaching, making wine and cheese, jellies and jams, fruitcakes and fudge, copying and preserving manuscripts and much more. At the time Saint Meinrad was founded, there was an urgent need to provide a native clergy for the German-speaking Catholics who had settled in southern Indiana. The seminary at Saint Meinrad has a distinguished history. The need for well-educated, holy priests is as great today as it was 150 years ago, and the monks of Saint Meinrad, working hand-in-hand with co-workers, continue to faithfully implement the program of priestly formation prescribed by the Holy See and by the United States Conference of Catholic Bishops.

At Saint Meinrad, I learned what it takes to form priests for the Church. I served as a teacher, a spiritual director and a seminary rector for nearly all of my 23 years as a monk and priest of Saint Meinrad. (For many years, I also had the privilege of serving as an advisor to the Pontifical College of Sant' Anselmo, the Benedictine university in Rome.) Thank God for this double-preparation for my ministry as bishop. Saint Meinrad helped me grow as a man of prayer, and it taught me the work of priestly formation. Both are essential to a bishop's life and ministry. Both prepared me to serve the Church in West Tennessee for five years and the Church in Central and Southern Indiana for nearly 20 years.

Because of my experience at Saint Meinrad, I was asked to lead the committee of bishops responsible for revising the Program of Priestly Formation (PPF) that applies standards developed by the Holy See to the particular circumstances of the Church in the United States. It was a great privilege for me to work closely with other bishops in developing the norms that guide seminary faculty and staff in all regions of our country as they seek to prepare men for service to the Church. Priestly formation involves a multifaceted process of educating the whole man for service to the Church as a priest. This includes forming the human, spiritual, intellectual, pastoral and community dimensions of each seminarian—bringing him to maturity in each area and preparing him for a lifelong process of continuing priestly formation. It's a complex and challenging process that is made more difficult by today's climate of secularism and relativism, but the rewards are truly worth the effort!

Blessed Pope John Paul II encouraged bishops to be personally involved in the formation of their future priests. I thank God that my years at Saint Meinrad prepared me so well for this critical responsibility.

In my 25 years as a bishop and archbishop, I have ordained many priests. Conferring the sacrament of holy orders is one of the greatest joys of my ministry as a bishop. However, I need to say that I would like to administer the sacrament of holy orders to a lot more priests! God calls young men to become seminarians, but these days it is not easy to hear his call. There are many distractions and not much encouragement. That makes it especially important for all of us to pray for vocations (and for our seminarians and priests).

Prayer and work. I was truly blessed to learn about both from the monks of Saint Meinrad. They taught me to prefer nothing to the love of Christ and to dedicate my life to the work of God (prayer) and to the great apostolate of priestly formation. As a monk, a priest and a bishop, I have tried to be faithful to the monks' teaching and example. May God bless Saint Meinrad!

CHAPTER FIFTEEN

STEWARDSHIP AND DEVELOPMENT

At the time I began my service as archbishop of Indianapolis, I inherited several studies and planning processes commissioned by my predecessor and good friend, Archbishop Edward T. O'Meara. On my desk, literally, were several stacks of reports and recommendations for parish staffing, Catholic education, urban ministry and Catholic Charities. All called for some kind of action by the new archbishop and all required the investment of significant dollars.

Fortunately, my years as president-rector at Saint Meinrad prepared me well in the challenging areas of planning and development. Saint Meinrad Archabbey and Seminary have been committed to development for nearly 50 years, and are recognized leaders among religious communities and seminaries in these important aspects of organizational leadership. I put what I learned about development at Saint Meinrad into practice in the Diocese of Memphis with very positive results. The Archdiocese of Indianapolis presented me with new challenges—and new opportunities—to prove that "best practices" in planning and development can (and should) be applied successfully to the pastoral governance of a Catholic diocese.

Effective development starts with a clear understanding of an organization's mission and priorities. In the Church, we do not "invent" these. Our mission and most fundamental priorities have already been given to us. At the same time, pastoral leaders in every generation are called to express the Church's mission and priorities in new language (the "new evangelization") and to develop action strategies that respond to the particular needs and circumstances of every time and place.

If you go to the website of the Archdiocese of Indianapolis (www.archindy.org), you'll find our mission statement. With a few minor changes, it is the same as it was when we first developed it 20 years ago:

> We, the Church in central and southern Indiana, called to faith and salvation in Jesus Christ in the Roman Catholic tradition, strive to live the Gospel by:
> - Worshiping God in word and sacrament
> - Learning, teaching, and sharing our faith
> - Serving human needs.
>
> We commit ourselves to generosity and to the responsible use of our spiritual and material resources.

I wanted our mission statement to be brief—so that people in all regions of the archdiocese could remember it. In fact, in my early days, I challenged the staff at the Catholic Center to memorize our mission statement. I kiddingly said that anyone who couldn't repeat it to me correctly would owe me a quarter. (I never collected any quarters!)

As part of our strategic planning effort, we also identified a series of fundamental values that were to guide all archdiocesan and parish activities. These have also remained fairly constant over the past 20 years—largely because they represent principles that are essential to the practice of our faith. As listed on the archdiocesan website, our values include:

- Prayer and spiritual growth
- Lifelong learning and sharing our faith
- Parish and family, the individual and community
- Compassion and respect for human life and all creation
- Justice and consistent moral standards
- Pro-active leadership and shared responsibility
- Vital presence in urban, suburban, and rural neighborhoods
- Stewardship.

I'm proud of the various planning efforts that we engaged in during my nearly 20 years as archbishop. We tried always to be faithful to the mission, values and priorities we received from the Universal Church, but we also worked hard to "discern the signs of the times" and to be pro-active and visionary in our anticipation of the future ministry needs of our people.

When I think about the challenges we face in carrying on the mission of Christ in our local Church, I think a lot about our holy founders.

One of many striking features about the life of Mother Theodore Guérin (now St. Theodora) is the courage of her faith. She put her life on the line for what she believed. St. Theodora didn't have to risk her life crossing the stormy Atlantic Ocean several times on ships that were minimally seaworthy. Nor, at the time, did she have to establish her community in the woods of primitive western Indiana. She did not have the money and teachers to establish schools for the poor, but she started them with conviction and prayer. She risked much and compensated with hard work and prayer even while in very poor health. We and countless others are the beneficiaries of her courageous faith and action.

The Servant of God Bishop Simon Bruté had been offered the position of physician to the French imperial court by Napoleon. He turned it down. Later, as a new priest, he was offered the position of court chaplain by Napoleon. Instead, Father Bruté chose to become a missionary in the new world. He could have lived a life of material comfort, but he chose rigorous missionary life in the most difficult circumstances. He also did so in poor health. It is likely that he already suffered from tuberculosis when he sailed down the Ohio River to take up his mission as bishop of the new diocese of Vincennes (now the Archdiocese of Indianapolis).

Under the leadership of Bishop Bruté, the Catholic Church in Indiana took root. He had not wanted to become a bishop. Yet, we and countless others are the beneficiaries of his courageous faith and humble obedience.

It is important to reflect on the fact that the vast majority of us Catholics enjoy worship and the availability of the sacraments, religious education and other aspects of parish life in facilities we did not pay for.

Even if at present we happen to be members of a new or expanding parish and have contributed to one of several archdiocesan and parish campaigns that have been held during the past 20 years, we were probably reared in a parish where the facilities and services were handed down from past generations. We all enjoy the fruit of the blood, sweat, tears and money of past generations; we have a responsibility to hand on to future generations the fruit of our generosity. In doing so, we are only acknowledging that everything comes from the hand of a most generous God and belongs to him.

An ancient Hebrew tradition teaches that almsgiving restores God's right order in the world, for through it we redistribute his gifts according to his plan. A proper understanding of stewardship reminds us that even those things we "own" are ultimately not truly ours, but gifts from God to be shared.

A tithe—a "gift" to the Church—is really a response to God's generosity, a recognition that the standard for giving is set by him who holds back nothing from us. We humbly admit that even our "hard-earned money" is a gift from God.

During my time as archbishop of Indianapolis, we conducted two archdiocesan-wide capital campaigns and several targeted fundraising efforts for specific purposes. These campaigns for the urgent, and growing, capital, endowment and ministry needs of the local Church provided us with opportunities prayerfully to measure our stewardship and "to return God's gifts to the Lord with increase."

Of course, stewardship is about a lot more than money. It involves our commitment to participate in the life of our local parish in prayer, sacrificing our precious time and putting our talents to work as best we can. Stewardship also includes a healthy regard for our churches, schools and other parish facilities: treating them as if they were our own home.

But stewardship is also about money. St. Theodora and Bishop Bruté risked their lives to obtain financial resources so that the mission of Christ's Church could take root and eventually flourish in our archdiocese. Our courageous pioneers of faith knew very well that the Church and her mission live in the real world. We can do no less.

The circumstances of our day make our ministries difficult to maintain, to foster and to develop with the faith and vision of our holy founders. We have many advantages and blessings our parents and grandparents in faith never had or could even envision. But with these advances have come contemporary forms of poverty. We do well to pray to our founding patrons, asking them to help us be courageous in faith as they were—and to work hard for the benefit of our children and generations to come.

I like to reflect on the obligation of being good stewards by reflecting on the spiritual connection between the Eucharist and stewardship. There is a connection that we can trace back to the beginnings of the Church.

The principle is clear. All baptized Catholics, wealthy and not so wealthy, educated and uneducated, should all be received in the community at Eucharist with the same welcome and respect, and all should share. The ministry of the Church, above all sacramental ministry, is not reserved only to those who are blessed with more personal and financial resources.

This is why collections of money for the poor have been taken up in assemblies of the faithful from the very origins of the Church. All kinds of scriptural references attest to the fact. It was perhaps best expressed by St. Paul's conviction that we cannot share the Eucharist while refusing to share our daily bread.

St. Paul goes one step further when he applies the word liturgy to the ministry of love and of fellowship, which is made concrete in the collection of gifts, including money. He uses the term "liturgy" *(leiturgia)*, which he says in turn leads to an outpouring of thanksgiving to God (Rom 15:27; 2 Cor 9:12f).

Writing to the Romans, St. Paul said, "I must take a present of money to the saints in Jerusalem, since Macedonia and Achaia have decided to send a generous contribution to the poor among the saints at Jerusalem. A generous contribution as it should be since it is really repaying a debt; the pagans who share the spiritual possessions of these poor people have a duty to help them with temporal possessions" (Rom 15:25-27).

In his second letter to the Corinthians, St. Paul wrote: "The one who provides seed for the sower and bread for food will provide you with all the seed you want and make the harvest of your good deeds a larger one, and made richer in every way, you will be able to do all the generous things which, through us, are the cause of thanksgiving to God. For doing this holy service *(leiturgia)* is not only supplying all the needs of the saints, but it is also increasing the amount of thanksgiving that God receives. By offering this service, you show them what you are, and that makes them give glory to God for the way you accept and profess the gospel of Christ, and for your sympathetic generosity for them and for all. And their prayers for you, too, show how they are drawn to you on account of all the grace that God has given you. Thanks be to God for his inexpressible gift" (2 Cor 9:10-15).

I bring this connection of worship and generous sharing to the forefront to remind us that our generous stewardship mirrors the teaching of St. Paul and, in fact, finds its Christian roots in this ancient tradition. Our generosity gives glory to God, and it helps the poor among the "saints" of our local Church in central and southern Indiana and throughout our nation and the world.

In 1992, the year I was installed as archbishop of Indianapolis, we bishops of the United States issued a pastoral letter on Christian stewardship titled "Stewardship: A Disciple's Response." A summary of the letter teaches that Jesus calls us to be disciples, and that call includes our decision to follow Jesus no matter what the cost (cf. the United States Catholic Catechism for Adults, pp. 450-452).

The stewardship pastoral reminds us that the Bible contains a profound message about the stewardship of material creation. We are stewards of creation. Our physical labor, the trades and professions, the arts and sciences, our work, is a participation in the stewardship of creation.

We are also called to be stewards of vocation. Each of us and all of us are called by God to make a difference in our world. Our response is an act of stewardship.

The fifth precept of the Church reminds us that we are stewards of the Church, and there are practical implications to Christ's ministry that make real demands on our time, talent and treasure (our financial resources) as baptized Christians and disciples of Jesus Christ. We are co-workers in the mission of proclaiming and cooperating in Christ's redemptive work. All of us have our role as stewards of Christ's mission.

Looking back on my 25 years as a bishop and archbishop, I can honestly say that my priorities remained constant—even as they took on different forms in response to particular needs and circumstances. What are these priorities?

Prayer was (and still is) my first priority. I love the celebration of the sacraments. Ordination to the priesthood is always memorable. I enjoy celebrating the Rite of Election of the Rite of Christian Initiation of Adults and the sacrament of confirmation. The dedication of new churches is awesome.

Educating seminarians has been a top priority. I pray that establishing Bishop Simon Bruté College Seminary at Marian College (now University) in Indianapolis will continue to be a blessing for the archdiocese and the Church.

Teaching is a priority that was given to me by Blessed Pope John Paul II when he first called me to be a bishop. I truly enjoyed writing my weekly column for *The Criterion*. The Holy Father also asked me to accept an important assignment as a Consultor for the Vatican Congregation of the Clergy and as his representative to the Council on Christian Unity sponsored by the Christian Church (Disciples of Christ).

Protecting our children is a critically important priority for me and for all bishops today. The ordeal of sexual abuse among clergy was certainly an unexpected one. I think our archdiocese responded appropriately when we learned about allegations of misconduct or abuse by Church personnel, but we can never slacken our efforts to prevent abuse and respond pastorally to those who have been harmed by the actions of a few very disturbed individuals.

A bishop is called to be a spiritual father to his priests, and I take this priority quite seriously. I worry about many of our priests who carry the burden of multiple parishes and assignments. Increasing the number of our seminarians is a challenge in our culture. Presiding at the funerals of nine priests in one year, 2005, was quite sad. As a Church, we need to pursue with even greater creativity and resources the finding of more vocations to the priesthood for the good of the Church and to provide for our hard-working priests. I pray for the help of our founding bishop, Simon Bruté, in this endeavor. He started with virtually no resources.

Catholic education has always been one of my top priorities. It is very hard work to maintain many of our Catholic schools. I am concerned about securing and maintaining fine Catholic schools and religious formation for the future. I continue to plead for St. Theodora's intercession in this area.

Having to eliminate many positions at the Catholic Center for financial reasons was not only difficult for me but for many others. We raised millions of dollars during my time as archbishop, but somehow there never seemed to be enough to meet the challenging needs of our mission. As with so many other things, I had to trust that God's providence would provide what we needed to proclaim Christ's Gospel and do the work of the Church faithfully in this place and time!

After 25 years as a bishop and archbishop, it's very clear to me that my "legacy" is not mine to determine. Future history will judge how successful I have been at shepherding the two dioceses entrusted to my care by Blessed Pope John Paul II. I pray that the faith and holiness of our people have deepened under my pastoral care. For my part, I tried to be a man of prayer and to trust in the sacramental grace of the office.

The fullness of the sacrament of holy orders makes all the difference.

For the rest, I had to rely on the goodness of the priests and people who assisted me in serving as pastor, priest and teacher in the person of Christ. I doubted myself occasionally, but I never doubted that the grace of Christ would sustain me in carrying out his work.

I would like to conclude this chapter, and these memories and reflections on my 25 years as a bishop and archbishop, with a quote from Pope Benedict XVI, which I believe says it all better than I can:

> *This is precisely what we mean when we call the ordination of priests a sacrament: ordination is not about the development of one's own powers and gifts. It is not the appointment of a man as a functionary because he is especially good at it, or because it suits him, or simply because it strikes him as a good way to earn his bread; it is not a question*

*of a job in which someone secures his own liveli-
hood by his own abilities, perhaps in order to rise
later to something better.*

*Sacrament means: I give what I myself cannot
give; I do something that is not my work; I am on a
mission and have become the bearer of that which
another has committed to my charge. … This very
self-expropriation for the other and selflessness that
are essential to the priestly ministry can lead to
authentic human maturity and fulfillment.*

When I first received the call to be a bishop, I was
surprised by grace. That same grace (the love of Christ)
has guided me, and sustained me, during the past
25 years in personal and ecclesial crises, in moments of
deep sorrow and in times of great joy.

I thank God for the gift of his grace. I hope to remain
open to it, and surprised by it—until I see him face-to-
face in our heavenly home.

AFTERWORD

This book was the result of a team effort. I must say thank you to the following:

- Caryn and Don Mucci for their truly generous support for this publication
- Dan Conway, the super editor, and his friend and colleague Bill Bruns
- Marge and Charlie Buechlein for their excellent choice in photographs
- Anne Wilmes, keeper of the family's photographic archives
- Grace Buechlein, a tireless proof reader
- Mark Mucci, a God-sent typist and friend
- Cardinal Francis George for his thoughtful contribution to this publication while dealing with his own health issues.

And to all who continue to support me with their prayers.

+Daniel Mark Buechlein, O.S.B.

Seeking the Face of the Lord

A Bishop and his Priests

verwhelmed with the realization that he shares the fullness of the Priesthood of Christ, the bishop envisions his own relationship with his priests after no other pattern than that of the Eternal High Priest with His apostles, as portrayed in the Gospel. It is a humbling responsibility that he shoulders when he becomes the Ordinary of a diocese. + *Joseph Cardinal Ritter - 1954*

Made in the USA
Middletown, DE
31 January 2018